PRAISE FOR *Of Mess and Moxie*

A NOTE FROM JEN HATMAKER

The most important readers to me are my actual readers because I am a literal person. While I can appreciate celebrity endorsements, well, as I explained in the intro for *Moxie*: "This one's for the girls." The opinions I cherish belong to my real girls—real readers, real women who read this book from cover to cover. With great affection, I give you endorsements from the girls who volunteered to help launch my last book then accidentally stuck around, basically became a little church, and showed up strong not just for this book but for each other and definitely for me— Jen the person, not just Jen the author. They are the friends you wished lived next door. Here is what they thought of *Moxie*:

"I see myself so clearly in Jen's stories that I feel spied on."
—ALLISON PICKETT, mom of four wild ones, the loudest and palest person in the room, ravenous for good books but mostly cake

"Never have I read a book that spoke to so many of my own fears or anxieties about being a wife, a daughter, or a believer."
—JACEY R. NORDMEYER

"The perfect blend of hilarious and touching. Jen Hatmaker's poignant insights are a breath of fresh air for every woman trying to navigate the Christian life in this age of impossible expectations."
—BARBARA SEIDLE

"Freeing and yet encouraging. It's time to free ourselves of the bondage in which we've placed ourselves and rest: rest in His goodness and in the goodness of others."
—AMILEE SANDERS

"Jen Hatmaker proves once again that she is *for* us, and she gets us. This is the type of book that makes you want to get on the phone with friends and say, 'Here, let me read this to you.'"
—HOLLY WAUGH, writer, blogger, lover of Jesus, Hot Mess but full of all the moxie I need

"Makes you feel like you are sitting on Jen's front porch, drinking a glass of wine, eating chips and salsa, and having conversations that have you crying at one moment, laughing the next, and then lastly screaming, 'Let there be Moxie! All is well.'"

—GWENDOLYN HOWES, lover of fine wine, craft beer, and food that she doesn't cook, spark plug that organizes and is always going to Carolina in her mind

"Reading this book is like sitting on the porch with a friend who looks you straight in the eye and says, 'Me too, I've been there, and here's what I've learned.' And those are my favorite kind of friends."

—JENNIFER WILLERTON

"Jen Hatmaker is America's girlfriend. She is right there at the sidelines, high-fiving us as we run our race and cheering us on as we live our messy lives."

—ABBIE MABARY

"I have laughed hysterically. Out loud. In public. I have cried big weepy tears. Out loud. In public. Moxie is refreshing: an author being raw, unguarded, and real."

—MORGAN JOHNSON

"This sixty-something is over the moon in love with *Of Mess and Moxie*! If you're a woman with a beating heart, this book's for you."

—LINDA HIBNER, a Jesus-Made-Me-Righteous Chick, Russ's girl, Everyone's Nana, and a 4th Act start-again writer

"I highlighted phrases, dog-eared pages, underlined passages, attached post-it notes, and wrote exclamation marks in the margins because so much of it spoke to me. Jen has so much love for women . . . and that love comes through on every page."

—KRISTI MCCLELLAN

"Every chapter left me wanting more. I will shout to the heavens and from all the rooftops in Oklahoma to buy this book. Don't stop, Jen, keep it going—we need more Moxie in our Mess."

—HOLLY JACKSON

"Full of kindly advice, straight talk about everything from parenting to religion, and some pretty delicious recipes. Jesus loves you, Jen loves you, and if you don't love yourself before reading this book, you will by the time you're done."

—KELLY MEEHAN

"Jen's observations are both witty and insightful—who else can explain why it's okay to grieve the atrocities in Syria yet still obsess over *Gilmore Girls*? A gem that you'll want to share with everyone you know."

—MINDY CHRISTIANSON, English teacher, #boymom, and lover of books and coffee

"Has heart, passion, a little bit of mess, and a whole lot of moxie. Jen Hatmaker is the friend we all wish we could meet for coffee. With her trademark honesty she relates her experiences in the church, in friendships, in family, and on television, with biblical truths and encouragement for all her sisters around the world. This one's for the girls, indeed. Moxie on, Jen."

—PATTIE REITZ

"This book had me in such hysterical laughter that my husband kept reading over my shoulder and laughing along with me."

—CLAIRE MUMMERT, mom, wife, hobby collector, amateur theologian, baker, and pursuer of sarcasm

"I laugh out loud, husband says, 'You're reading *Of Mess And Moxie*?' Same conversation happens with the tears. "

—BARBARA KNEPPER

"This book reads like a family reunion—the kind you *want* to be a part of. You're in the family. Dive on in and make yourself comfortable."

—REBECCA MILLER

"I dropped everything and read it in twenty-four hours. This book not only made me feel all my feelings, but reminded me that all my feelings are gifts from God. Thank you, Jen Hatmaker! You are the Queen!"

—DANIELLE JOSEPHINE DEWITT

"No matter age, social status, or beliefs, you will be challenged and changed by this book. *Of Mess and Moxie* will make you ugly cry, it will make you laugh, and most importantly it will speak life to you."

—HEATHER GERWING

"Jen tells us that we have not failed or done something wrong when things get messy. It is at this point our inner moxie comes out and we push on and show the world what we have inside of us."

—SHANNON IMEL, wife for eleven years, mom for eight years, massive sweet tooth, loves to laugh, digs HGTV and Food Network, and loves to take naps

"Jen's words just call out to be underlined, circled, arrowed, asterisked, and amen-ed all over the place. You're going to need a fancy new pen or five."

—BETHANY BEAMS, mother of a five-year-old; singer of the third harmony part; lover of people, stories, Honeycrisps, Hamilton, and naps

"Reading through Jen's *Of Mess and Moxie* did something to me. I'm not even sure what all that is yet, but I can sense something really significant and life changing from it. I felt validated, valued, and cared for in the very words she spoke over me."

—JACLYN PARSONS

"This book is a treasured gift for my misfit soul."

—KELLY SHANK, writer, frequent flyer to Guatemala, wannabe world traveler, wife, and mama

"All the feels, all the good, all the bad, and how to love people, yourself, and Jesus thrown into one delicious book. This. Is. Everything."

—JODI FLETCHER

"For all of you who've felt isolated in a lonely corner of Christianity like I have, this book is for you. There is beauty in your mess, and Jen is here to show it to you with her signature blend of irreverence and poignant grace. Her best work yet."

—KIMBERLY POOVEY, writer, speaker, educator, and over-caffeinated toddler mom

"Jen doesn't for a second let you think she has it all together, but I promise you will leave this book feeling empowered to go love your friends and enemies with all you've got."

—ANNA PRICE, Denton, Texas; loves the church, justice, and friends around her dinner table

"I found myself not being entertained by this book. Yet again, Jen had found places in my heart that needed attention, and this time around, it was painful. Jen's observations met me where I am."

—MELINDA WEDDING

"It's fun, witty, serious, sensitive, loving, encompassing, tender, sobering, easy to read, and heart-wrenching—all at the same time. I can't imagine a woman who can't find herself nodding along, saying, 'Me, too!'"

—CAROLYN HARPER

"From the moment I turned the first page, I felt like I was reading a letter from a trusted friend. The kind of friend who knows exactly what you're going through because she's been there too."

—LISA BARTELT, Pennsylvania; wife, mom, writer, Woman in Progress

"Jen serves it all up with a large dose of humor, the wisdom of someone twice her age, and the knack for storytelling that keeps you wanting more. Definitely on my gift list for women ages fourteen–eighty!"

—ERIN NEEDHAM, wife, mother, teacher, and procrastinator extraordinaire

"Got me kicked out of bed for my inability to stifle laughter! The beginning drew me in, the middle made me laugh, and the last four chapters left me wanting more. Another JHat masterpiece!"

—NICHOLE CARRABBIA, Air Force wife and homeschool mom by day; writer, reader, Netflix and Fallon watcher by night; Jesus-lover, mess-maker, and moxie-seeker always

"There is a vulnerability in Jen's stories that calls us to be done with 'faking' it. Both a breath of fresh air and a sigh of relief."

—ALLISON BALL

"She switches seamlessly between humorous, inspirational, and memoir-style essays. Somehow, she manages to relate to women (and men!) in every stage of life, making us laugh, cry, and draw nearer to God. I cannot recommend this book highly enough."

—RUTH SZPUNAR from Indiana

"Chronicles Jen's own pilgrim progress in seasons of growth and change. Jen's message: You are not stuck. You are not broken. You are not a victim."

—CAROL FRUGÉ

"Jen's pleading that it's never too late to become stronger and 'you don't have to be who you first were' gives readers permission to forgive themselves and live a life worthy of God's mercy and grace. She does this with self-deprecating and coffee-spitting humor about family, friends, marriage, Netflix, and exercise."

—SUZANNE REES, thirty-years-a-wife, empty-nest mom, rescuer-of-shelter-animals, just coming into my own with this Christianity thing

"My book is dog-eared, underlined, and highlighted. It brings hope, laughter, joy, and yet challenges you. Well done, Jen. You are loved, cherished, wanted, and treasured."

—REBECCA LACOUNT, Slice of Heaven

"Jen Hatmaker lives out of abundance. There is no room for scarcity. Always room for others. In her writing she has a way of making you feel like you don't have to go find a different table. You belong right here."

—TERRI FULLERTON

"Dances through seasons of life with reflections on faith, family, friendship, and the hoods: childhood, siblinghood, spousehood, and parenthood. Jen's words encourage, inspire, comfort, and refresh. I want to come back to them time and again and soak in them like a bubble bath."

—HEATHER BRADY, Austin, Texas

"I've long fashioned myself a bit of a Junior Jesus. I caught my reflection in the looking glass and realized I make a much better sister and friend than I do a superhero. Thanks for encouraging me to take off the mask of 'rescuer' and instead brush my teeth and throw my hair in a top knot as sister-friend."

—KARIANN LOY LESSNER, wife, momma, friend, minister for children and families, spotty-blogger, fairy-godmother to many

"For the husbands: Your wife may very well shout out a 'hallelujah' or two, and she may also cry in relief and/or solidarity. Embrace it, buddy. You love her in the Mess of life and admire her for her Moxie, so this book could not be more perfect!"

—BETHANY MARLOW, Castle Rock, Colorado

"The reminder we all need right now to love each other well. Jen's words flow from a trusted source: favorite neighbor, loyal friend, crazy aunt, and constructive counselor all rolled into one."

—LINDSAY K. EVANS

"Jen Hatmaker opened the doors and windows for all the people. She weaves her story in such a way that it is easy to imagine you are just gathered for an afternoon chat on the porch. She just keeps showing up to shine her light and beat her drum."

—PAMELA WESTVOLD JUSTUS, love warrior, peacemaker, ever hopeful, Spirit-filled educator, messy creative, mostly joyful mom of three beautiful teens

"Another hilarious, wise, sobering, beautiful piece of literature. If you've read her work before, welcome back. It is exactly as awesome as you're expecting."

—ANNALIESE WINK, Grapevine, Texas

"I've tended to collect a mental stone of remembrance from each of my many messy moments. Once those stones begin to stack so high, it's difficult to see anything but the mess. *Of Mess and Moxie* came in like a wrecking ball, tearing down those walls and revealing the moxie I didn't even realize was there all along."

—ASHLEY DOYLE POOSER, a sleep-deprived, over-caffeinated mom of three and wannabe writer, generally flying by the seat of her pants in Atlanta

"My husband said he loved to hear my giggles as I read this book with delight. In between the giggles there were also tears. Jen has a way of doing that."

—KATIE CICCIONE, Atlanta by way of Chicago

"Just when I'm feeling that I'm too old to fit in, Jen assures me that the world 'needs my voice, my leadership, my presence . . . because no matter my age, I have a role to play. Sisterhood is lifelong.' You'll likely need a Kleenex when you read that last chapter, because *yes*, we are all capable of some serious Moxie even with our Mess. We can link arms and do incredible things."

—KIMBERLY WIDMER

"If you've ever felt left out, misunderstood, too much, or not enough, Jen's your girl."

—AUBREY STOUT, wife and mom, who happens to be named after a '70s soft rock song

"I read part of this book to my husband. He said, 'Oh, man. I need to go buy Brandon Hatmaker a beer.' He said this because Jen is so me. And she's so you. She's so all of us. That's what her books do; they connect us with laughter, struggle, and spirit. Read it, friend."

—EMILY DONEHOO, woman who writes at donehoo.blogspot.com

"I feel that Jen has found her voice. There is a strength, a maturity, in her words that comes only after struggle and pain. Jen navigates her growth with both humor and humility, owning her struggle, and gaining wisdom in the process."

—KAREN MCVEY, priest's wife, SAHM to seven babies, ages twenty-two to seven, lover of chocolate, queso, and wine

"No guilt allowed. Jen specializes in this recipe. It is her down-home, comfort-food specialty, folded into the stories of her life and the truths (both beautiful and not so) of modern-day Christianity."

—JESSICA BURROWS

"How an anthem for *all* women should be lived out: head held high, ready to use your moxie to do what Jesus called us to do: love our neighbor as ourselves—our true, messy, come-as-you-are, stay-a-while, laugh, cry, serve, encourage, loving selves."

—JENNIEMARIE CISNEROS, wife, mom, coffee-fueled storyteller, bookworm, child of God.

"Equal parts kick in the rear, punch in the gut, pat on the back, and stitch in the side. Chapter by chapter, Jen builds her case that God's love for us is wild enough to capsize our fears, deep enough to overcome our messes, and wide enough to include every Outcast and Other. "

—TAMARA SHOPE

"No matter the stage of life we are in, Jen sees us, welcomes us, and reminds us we are each doing the best we can, leaning on God and one another. Join us at the table: we won't be the same without you."

—KELLY JOHNSON, empty-nest drama mama, aficionado of all things brave

OF MESS
and MOXIE

Wrangling Delight Out of This
Wild and Glorious Life

JEN HATMAKER

NELSON
BOOKS

An Imprint of Thomas Nelson

Published in Nashville, Tennessee, by Nelson Books, an imprint of Thomas Nelson. Nelson Books and Thomas Nelson are registered trademarks of HarperCollins Christian Publishing, Inc.

Published in association with Yates & Yates, www.yates2.com.

Thomas Nelson titles may be purchased in bulk for educational, business, fund-raising, or sales promotional use. For information, please e-mail SpecialMarkets@ThomasNelson.com.

Scripture quotations are taken from the Holy Bible, New International Version®, NIV®. Copyright © 1973, 1978, 1984, 2011 by Biblica, Inc.® Used by permission of Zondervan. All rights reserved worldwide. www.zondervan. com. The "NIV" and "New International Version" are trademarks registered in the United States Patent and Trademark Office by Biblica, Inc.®

Any Internet addresses, phone numbers, or company or product information printed in this book are offered as a resource and are not intended in any way to be or to imply an endorsement by Thomas Nelson, nor does Thomas Nelson vouch for the existence, content, or services of these sites, phone numbers, companies, or products beyond the life of this book.

ISBN 978-0-7180-3184-8 (HC)
ISBN 978-0-7180-3186-2 (eBook)
ISBN 978-1-4041-0631-4 (custom)

Library of Congress Control Number: 2017933589

Printed in the United States of America

17 18 19 20 21   LSC   10 9 8 7 6 5 4 3 2 1

For my girlfriends, who have taught me more moxie than I could dream. You know exactly who you are. I could never, ever do this life without you. Not one day.

I am not afraid of storms for I am learning how to sail my ship.[1]

— *Louisa May Alcott*

CONTENTS

CONTENTS

INTRODUCTION

It has recently come to my attention that not everyone jammed to country music in the nineties. My lifespan that decade was from age sixteen to twenty-six, so those musicians literally sang me through high school, college, early marriage, and young motherhood. I entered the nineties as a junior in high school and left it married with two kids. I logged all those years in Kansas, Oklahoma, and Texas, so country music was our state genre, our shared anthem. I thought this was ubiquitous until my adult friends chastised me for favoring Garth over Nirvana. I obviously have friends in low places.

My Pandora station of choice to this living day is Trisha Yearwood. Faith, Alison, Shania, Martina, Jo Dee, The Chicks, Reba—these girls, with their high-waisted jeans and belly shirts— sang me through new independence and the sharp thrill of young adulthood. I cannot locate a memory during those years that isn't tied to their collective music.

One of my tip-top favorite artists was Martina McBride, who later gave us an anthem for the ages: "This One's for the Girls."

What I want to do is insert the lyrics here, but I would basically need Martina to drive to my house, hold my hand, recite the Constitution, and sign off in her own blood (lyric permissions are harder to secure than a date to prom with Bradley Cooper). Girls, download the song, grab a glass of wine, and remember why being a woman among women is a gift and a treasure.

In her beautiful tribute to sisterhood, Martina dedicates each verse to women in varying stages of life, decade by decade, identifying with them in all their angst, hopes, and glory. I belt this song out on the back of Brandon's motorcycle so passionately, he has to tap my leg lest I distract him with my performance.

In the tender spirit of Martina's love song to women from middle school to great-grandmotherhood, I want to welcome you to this book, this space, this sisterhood.

This is for all you girls about twenty-three. You're here, bursting into adulthood. We who are ahead of you are so glad you made it! We've been raising you, watching you, cheering you on. You are trying on this new grown-up suit, and it feels amazing and terrifying and thrilling and weird. *You* are in charge of you now. You're trotting out dreams and ideas, and none of them feels as simple as you imagined four years ago. Life is grittier and a wee bit less hospitable than you envisioned when the world was your oyster, protecting your dreams from harsher conditions.

But here you are. You are young and beautiful, fresh and energetic. It's your turn to begin a new story. You'll slog through entry-level jobs and sticky relationships and rent and health insurance just like we all did, and you'll make it, just like we all did. This one is for you. Listen to those of us twenty years ahead of you: This life is not a race or a contest, there is enough abundance to go around, your seat at the table is secure, and you have incredible gifts to offer. You are not in competition with your peers. Be a good sister. Be brave enough to take your place and humble enough to learn and share. We are so glad you are here. We believe in you, we love you, we are thrilled to welcome you to the tribe.

This is for all you girls around thirty-eight. You may be in the thick of the Family Years, and life is joyful and tedious and tender and bananas. You never knew you were capable of such juggling and feel like you get it right around 33 percent of the time. Marriage has worn a trusted groove, and also it is hard. You've relinquished young adult angst and narrowed in on your gifts, your preferences, the stuff that gets you out of bed in the morning and begs to be brought forth. But life is really crowded, so many need you, and sometimes the competing voices wear you out, wear you down. You have some really beautiful dreams; some of them are already realized, some are half-baked, some live privately in your secret stash of yearnings.

You've earned those laugh lines, those stretch marks, those pesky gray hairs. Your body has served you well; it has maybe even delivered whole human beings. But, in any case, it has carried you halfway through your life. This one is for you. I am your true sister, right here in the middle with you. I've watched you mother and sister and serve with such courage and loyalty, I can barely believe I get to claim this generation alongside you. You won't find a bigger fan than me. I am convinced there is nothing we cannot tackle, solve, endure, or dream. You're smart. Your work is meaningful, and it is mattering. I am proud of you, proud to belong to you. I believe in us.

This is for all you girls about fifty-nine. You've done it! You raised the kids, survived the crowded years, and five-plus decades of life look so good on you. Those of us coming up behind you are watching in awe. We see you with your beautiful faces and those hands that have accomplished so much. We are slow clapping, because you are our mentors and your example tells us that we, too, are going to make it. Your careers and achievements are heroic. You paved a lot of ground that we are now walking on confidently. You won battles that we no longer have to fight. You made a way for the women behind you. We honor you.

What is life after the next generation is raised and gone? I'm no psychic, but I'm guessing *one big party*. You're grandmothering now maybe—all the fun and none of the responsibility. Maybe it feels a little disorienting? I imagine after living certain roles for two or three decades, it might seem confusing to write a new chapter later in the game. This one is for you. I believe we never outgrow fresh dreams and courage, and I assure you we still need your voice, your leadership, your presence—now more than ever. It's never too late to become stronger. As long as we are breathing air, we have a role to play. Sisterhood is lifelong.

This is for all the girls. The ones who thought they'd be married by now but are still single, who thought they'd be mothers by now but aren't, who said they didn't want children and have four. The ones whose marriages didn't work, the ones who found love a second time. This is for the girls who are passionate, bold, assertive; those who are gentle, quiet, impossibly dear. It's for the decorated career slayer, the creative artist, the mom raising littles, the student in a dorm, the grandmother beginning a new venture. This is for the girls absolutely living their passions and those who want to desperately but feel stuck. This one is for church girls, party girls, good girls, wild girls (I am all four). This is for all of us.

We are spread out across geography, generations, and experiences, but we have two important things in common: mess and moxie. First, on *mess*: this word has gone a bit off the rails, I fear. When my last book, *For the Love*, came out, an older gal wrote a scathing, church-lady-finger-wagging article on it, calling me and my fellow sisthren "messy transparents," and she wasn't having it. Make of our reaction what you will, but the launch team and I howled! We messy transparents are just out mucking around in the pigpen of life apparently.

Messy, hard, disappointing, painful, shocking, exhausting, aggravating, boring. However you want to say it, life *is* messy. For all of us. I'm not making this up; I'm just saying it out loud. Your mess is normal, and it is okay to admit it. Pain is not exceptional or rare. If you've lived longer than five minutes, you already know this. Not because your particular brand of life is exceptionally punishing or you are doing everything exceptionally wrong, but because, as it turns out, this is how it is for everyone. This is the price of being a human on this planet; we get the glorious and the grueling, and surprisingly, the second often leads to the first. Trust this messy transparent who loves you. We are in the same boat.

We will endure discouragement, heartbreak, failure, and suffering. All of us. And more than once. And in more than one category. And in more than one season. But we are the very same folks who can experience triumph, perseverance, joy, and rebirth. More than once. And in more than one category. And in more than one season.

And that? That is *moxie*. Isn't that a delicious, dreamy word? Moxie. It is a throwback to women with pluck, with chutzpah, with a bit of razzle dazzle. It says: I got this . . . we got this together. It evokes a twinkle in the eye, a smidge of daring and stubbornness in the face of actual, hard, real, beautiful life. Moxie reaches for laughter, for courage, for the deep and important truth that women are capable of weathering the storm. We are not victims, we are not weak, we are not a sad, defeated group of sob sisters.

Yes, life is hard, but we are incredibly resilient. It is how God created us: He said, "Let there be moxie!" and it was good (paraphrased). We already have what we need. It is all inside, so waiting around for our circumstances to deliver our expected life is a waste of energy.

I'm convinced there is no such thing as Someday. You know the Someday I mean? The one where our dreams finally come true and life gets miraculously easier and we get off high center and all the things we imagined or envisioned or hoped for materialize? When that one critical piece is added or subtracted, when we are finally less busy, when a bunch of vague things come together and present us with the life we expected? I've learned that we don't outrun our circumstances, nor do we simply outlast them; we just trade them for new issues, new struggles, new challenges.

Let's not mourn the mess and forget our moxie.

Rather than waiting for the Someday life or, conversely, imagining our Someday life is in the rearview mirror and we'll never reclaim it, what if we embraced it all right now: all the hope, all the thrill, all the growth, all the possibility? What if everything is available to us right here in the middle of ordinary, regular life?

We have been warned that *ordinary* is less than, a sign of inferiority, an indicator that so much more awaits if we could just get the mix right. But the truth is, most of life *is* pretty ordinary, so it is precisely inside the ordinary elements, the same ones found the world over—career, parenting, change, marriage, community, suffering, the rhythms of faith, disappointment, being a good neighbor, being a good human—that an extraordinary life exists.

Someday is right now, in the life you already have.

Which contains plenty of mess but even more moxie.

May you find courage and God in these pages. I sincerely hope you throw your head back and guffaw out loud in public at least a few times; I love to make you laugh and I don't think humor is unimportant. I've tried to treat our tender spaces with great care, but if I barrel through or misspeak or leave out an important part of the story, the fault is mine and I beg your grace. Life is crazy gorgeous and crazy hard, and we don't mean to fail each other but we do, which is why Anne Lamott calls earth *Forgiveness School.*

You belong here; that is the short version of the story. God has given me a deep, almost painful love for this tribe. I think about you, I dream about you, I care about you, and my aim is to serve you until I die. If that feels dramatic, well, no one ever accused me of subtlety. Welcome. You are very loved here.

FOR THE GIRLS,

Jen

Many people between the ages of thirty and sixty—whatever their *stature* in the community and whatever their personal *achievements*—undergo what can truly be called a second journey. The second *journey* begins when we know we cannot live the afternoon of *life* according to the morning program.[1]

–BRENNAN MANNING

CHAPTER 1

UNBRANDED

Close your eyes, please, and imagine this graphic: Hot pink sunglasses with rhinestones at the corners, bright "sunbursts" popping off in dramatic fashion, and white swirled stars on a baby-blue background. It is colorful. It is bubbly. It is moderately-to-severely juvenile.

It was my first book cover.

I freaking loved it too. I remember thinking, *This is so me.* No stuffy book cover for this renegade! No woman standing in a meadow! No beach scene! No flowers! No, ma'am. This is 2005, and I will put a pair of sparkly retro sunglasses out into the literary world and state my arrival as a fresh new voice with style and, dare I say, *panache.*

Oh, my lordamercy.

Bless all my heart.

You guys, I cannot even muster the courage to read one paragraph of it now. I planned on combing through some of its content to cite as evidence, but I can't bring myself to open it. I can tell you it was incredibly earnest. Like, earnest enough to make you cringe all the way to Antarctica (it was titled *A Modern Girl's Guide to Bible Study*, you guys). I can tell you it wasn't well researched, because I wrote it when I was twenty-nine with dial-up Internet and half of one clue. I can tell you the stories were overwrought, forced into application, and included three times the words necessary. I can tell you it absolutely abused Christianese. When women occasionally report how it recently served them, it confirms my suspicion that God is still in the business of speaking through jackasses.

But, nonetheless, it was true to me and of me at the time.

It was my rhinestone sunglasses season.

Shortly after that and a few similar books later, I moved into a place of full spiritual deconstruction. God upended my family's life, and we moved from megachurch to missional church. Everything unraveled, and I was plagued by hard new questions I'd never asked, much less answered. I was tortured and undone and burning everything to the ground. My spiritual tension was at an all-time high, and my words were tinged with angst, disillusionment, skepticism, and no small amount of self-righteousness. I was pretty sure the American church was on the fast track to ruination and the poor "would always be among us" because Christians were a bunch of selfish nationalists with allegiance to Mammon. Delightful. I penned a whole book about it if you'd like a dose of anxiety with your morning coffee. Like I gently wrote: "Hey, here's something crazy: In the Word, poverty, widows, hunger—these are not metaphors. There are billions of lambs that literally need to be fed. With food."[1] It was a really fun time to be around me.

That was my *Interrupted* season.

Born from that place of critical analysis, I swung a big bat at consumerism for the next few years. I invited (forced) my family into a yearlong social experiment called *7* in which we evaluated and reduced our consumption of food, clothes, possessions, media and technology, spending, waste, and stress. And not like, *Hey family, let's have a little meeting about recycling,* but more like, *We are all going to wear the same seven pieces of clothing for a month (half-hearted* is not an adjective ever wasted on me).

We ate the same seven foods for a month, wore the same seven pieces of clothing for a month, gave away seven things a day for a month, eliminated seven forms of media, spent money in only seven places, and adopted seven practices to care for the earth. I mean, we did not even play. I reduced my closet by 80 percent. I constantly worried over ethical supply chains, the wealth gap, landfills, and the next doomed generation of Xbox fanatics. I was afraid to buy a twelve-dollar shirt for fear of hypocrisy. I wrote a book about our experimental mutiny, which was responsible for roughly one hundred thousand readers canceling their cable (I'm sorry, husbands).

That was my simplification season.

And here I am today. I carry less angst and am not caught in the grip of as much turmoil. I'm in a season of joy, honestly. After several years of spiritual upheaval, I've seized some contentment, and grace has worked its magic. When people read my books out of order, they are like, *Wait, what?* Looking back over the last ten years, I still embody vital pieces of every season—I am still passionately for the poor and crave a truly Good News church for the world—but I've also continually shifted forward in new ways, into different head spaces. There is a clear trajectory in my life through changing seasons marked by new ideas, new burdens, new focal points, and new leadership.

You know what that is? Good, right, healthy, alive.

I thought long and hard about how I wanted to start this book, this twelfth book, this next iteration of who I am and who we are together, dear reader. What opening note did I want? How do I want to launch these next few hours and days with you as you hold these pages and we create shared space together? And I decided my first words to you would be these:

You don't have to be who you first were.

That early version of yourself, that season you were in, even the phase you are currently experiencing—it is all good or purposeful or at least useful and created a fuller, nuanced you and contributed to your life's meaning, but you are not stuck in a category just because you were once branded that way. Just because something *was* does not mean it will *always be.*

Maybe part of your story involves heartache, abuse, struggle, loss, choices you wish you had back. Those are particularly sticky labels to unpeel. Those seasons tend to brand us permanently, at least to others, maybe especially to ourselves. Once we are that one thing, it is hard not to be. Whether self-imposed or foisted upon us, we are assessed through that specific lens: damaged, failure, addict, victim, broken, unhealthy, abuser, quitter, injured, frail. These identities stick long after they've lost their staying power. They are particularly grim ashes to rise from in beauty.

Someone dear to me was abused at a fragile age. The details unspeakable, the situation unfathomable. Without question, that abuse had the capacity to permanently wound. I sat this person down, mustered up every bit of authority I'd ever claimed in Jesus, and said, "This is not who you are. This happened to you, but it does not define you. You are not broken. You are not ruined. You are not destined to a lifetime of sexual dysfunction. You will become the exact person God intended all along, and you will be stronger in these fragile places than you were before it happened. This is a part of your story, not the end of it, and you will overcome. Not only that; you will *thrive.* If God is truly the strongest where we are the weakest, then He will win in this place."

You are far more than your worst day, your worst experience,

your worst season, dear one. You are more than the sorriest decision you ever made. You are more than the darkest sorrow you've
endured. Your name is not Ruined. It is not Helpless. It is not
Victim. It is not Irresponsible. History is replete with overcomers
who stood up after impossible circumstances and walked in freedom. You are not an anemic victim destined to a life of regret. Not
only are you capable, you have full permission to move forward
in strength and health.

And if you are prepared for a new, fresh season but others
refuse to let you grow into it, sister, shake the dust from your feet
and move on anyway. You may need to live a new story before
others are willing to bless it. Let them see you laugh again, come
back to life, dream new dreams, embrace healing. It can be difficult to *envision* a new start but impossible to *deny* one. This is
your work. No one can do it for you. God created us to triumph;
we are made in the image of Jesus, who has overcome the world.
We are never defeated, not even when all evidence appears to the
contrary. If you are still breathing, there is always tomorrow, and
it can always be new.

You don't have to be who you were.

Maybe it isn't a matter of conquering struggle but simply
growing forward in new ways. Sometimes these nuanced shifts
are even harder to navigate because they aren't born of pain or
loss, which are easier to quantify. Perhaps God is seeding you
with new vision, new ideas, different perspectives, or even enormous adjustments. It could be that you have changed your mind
or changed your position. Maybe that thing you loved has run its
course. Something doesn't have to be bad to be over. That season
has possibly given you everything it has to offer; it shaped and
developed you, it stretched and inspired you. You've deeply incorporated its lasting values, and it has been true to you and of you.
But now it's time to move forward to something new, different,

surprising, or risky. You might not necessarily be *leaving* one thing but *running toward* something else. G. K. Chesterton wrote: "A dead thing can go with the stream, but only a living thing can go against it."[2] Change means you're alive, my friend.

Perhaps *you* are the one resisting change, imagining your best days are behind you. Maybe the narrative in your head sounds like: *I used to be braver, I used to be thinner, I used to be needed, I used to love my career, I used to have a happy marriage, I used to love my body, my season, my life. The days ahead can never compare with the days behind.* It could be that you didn't ask for the change you face: you didn't sign up for your husband's affair, getting fired, a child's illness, infertility, mental illness. Since you didn't initiate or want this change, it feels like a deal breaker, a joy stealer, and you're tempted to throw in the towel. Girl, no. Just NAH.

We can retain irreplaceable lessons and core values from every season. We are not entirely rebranded with each new season; we simply build the next layer. Throughout transitions, we embody permanent virtues and become deeply shaped, and as a testament to our design, we are capable of preserving the best of each season while rejecting the worst. The human heart is shockingly resilient.

By choice or by force, people grow and evolve, which can be incredibly healthy but not always met with approval. We usually like others, and sometimes even ourselves, to remain the same, treading the familiar paths, the ones we know, the ones we're used to. Change makes us nervous in general. It is so tempting to interpret *new* as an indictment against the *old*, but that is an incomplete story.

Two thoughts: It is incredibly tempting to disparage people who didn't "change" with us. I have criticized the words of others when the same words came out of my own mouth just two years earlier, which is incredibly un-self-aware. Human insecurity wants everyone right where we are, in the same head space at the same time. We want to progress (and digress) at a comparable rate: *Everyone be into this thing I'm into! Except when I'm not. Then everyone be cool.*

We need to get better at permission and grace. What is right for us may not be right for everyone, and we don't have to burn down the house simply because we've moved our things out. Other good folks probably still live there, and until one minute ago, we did too. We can bless the honorable parts of that house and express sincere gratitude for what we learned under its roof. It is unwise and shortsighted to isolate the remaining inhabitants, because there is a lot of life left, and as it turns out, we are all still neighbors.

Second, it is also human nature to disparage people when *they* move into a new season. Whether shifting forward or "being left," the impulse to discredit remains. I get it. We like our people to stay in the house.

My family worked steadily for six years to relocate collectively to Austin. Brandon and I moved here first, then one sister, then my parents, then the in-laws, then everyone else. Every last extended family member was finally in the same city, and we were living the dream. The family compound! We did it! So when my sister Lindsay announced she was quitting her office job and moving to NYC to go to culinary school, we all freaked out and heaped discouragement on her decision:

What?!
It's too expensive!
You have nowhere to live!
It's a concrete jungle!
Why would you leave Austin?
You already have a college degree!
Go to culinary school here!

After a few weeks of this opposition, she finally sat us down and explained how lonely and unsupported she felt and how our disapproval was crushing.

Record scratch.

The thing was, we really just wanted her to stay in our house. That was the root of our cynicism. It was a simple matter of feeling left behind. Without considering the impact of our criticism, our aim was to keep the house intact. But it is shortsighted to isolate people who move to a new house, because that neighbor thing is sturdier than we think. A healthy community includes a lot of homes. This move was right and good and healthy for my sister, and we ultimately sent her off with our blessings.

You do not have to be who you were, who you have been. If you have a dream brewing, I hope to throw light all over it. If you encounter a new idea or perspective, I hope you feel free enough to consider it. If you need to bury an old label, girl, here is a shovel. You can care about new things and new people and new beginnings, and until you are dead in the ground, you are not stuck. If you move with the blessing of your people, marvelous. But even if you don't, this is your one life, and fear, approval, and self-preservation are terrible reasons to stay silent, stay put, stay sidelined.

You are not pigeonholed into a brand; that is not the way God works. He is on the move, which means, if we are paying attention, we are on the move with Him. It's so exciting! Possibility and adventure and love and life await us all. These are the calling cards of the kingdom, and they are ours. There is literally nothing we cannot consider, no new season we cannot embrace.

We still retain the rights to every important thing we learned along the way; those layers count and make up the whole of who we are. We have important memories from every house—some painful, some instructive, some delightful, some necessary. But how thrilling to realize that even now God is designing a new blueprint, tailor-made, and His creativity extends to the very trajectory of our lives.

Onward, sisters.

There is no way to
be a *perfect* mother,
and a million ways
to be a *good* one.[1]

—JILL CHURCHILL

CHAPTER 2

MOMS, WE'RE FINE

Except for a year or two in my parenting tenure, I've always been a working mom. Sometimes part time, sometimes from home, sometimes full time, but always working. With five kids, this means putting my head down and *handling it* while they are at school. Which also means I am not a weekly volunteer in their classrooms or the teacher workroom or any of that biz, because, as I have to remind my kids constantly, I have a job. This technicality never seems to connect with my spawn:

CHILD: Can you bring me Chick-fil-A for lunch?
ME: No, son, I'm working.
CHILD: Doing what? What do you even do?
ME: OH MY GOSH.

So I prioritize the special stuff: parties, field trips, programs, and award assemblies. However, while I'm pretty decent at getting the dates right, the details often turn into white noise. If I assimilate the date, the starting time, and the entry fee, that feels like a mothering win. This is the best I can do. ("I'm so sorry, but I cannot make the class banner for the parade. Why not? Oh, because I don't want to.")

Anyway, when Sydney was in fourth grade, she had a field trip to . . . something somewhere. Listen, I am good at other things. I knew driving parents had to follow the buses pulling out at 8:30 a.m. Great. I showed up to the school parking lot with all the other moms and two or three SAHDs and proceeded to return phone calls in the car, which all my girlfriends and colleagues know is the only time I talk on the phone. (Leave me a message and be prepared to never hear from me again, or perhaps possibly next Friday when I'm driving to the airport. But probably never.)

Two buses pulled out, and I got in line behind the other cars and put my mind on autopilot as we headed south down I-35. Three phone calls later, I started thinking, *Good night! Where are we going? What was this field trip? Something about government? Or maybe astronomy?* I pulled alongside the buses just to make sure I hadn't lost the caravan, but sure enough, our school name was emblazoned on the side.

After an hour and a half, we pulled into the San Antonio Zoo, which I surely didn't remember as a pertinent detail. I parked, sauntered over to the buses, and watched the entire fifth grade contingency pile out. Which was delightful. For fifth graders. But my kid was in *fourth*, and I had inadvertently followed the wrong bus—not to the correct destination ten minutes from school, but to *another city*.

I will not type out the curses I screamed, as they are unbecoming even to a trucker, but I sped eighty miles an hour to the correct location after despertexting (desperate texting) my girlfriend something that sounded like, "Where the *&#@! are you guys??" I missed the entire movie (Ah! A movie! About whales! At the IMAX!) and finally caught up with the fourth graders at the after-picnic in the park. Helpfully, I'd also promised my friend Becky to be the surrogate field trip mom for her daughter, since Becky couldn't go.

So I found my two forlorn charges eating their sad sandwiches, motherless, worried that I had either wrecked or run off to Mexico. While my fellow elementary school moms were sprawled on the ground, guffawing about my driving six zip codes away, Sydney said, "Mom, me and Makenna were like the orphaned baby whales in the movie."

Jesus, be a fence.

Motherhood often feels like a game of guilt management; sometimes the guilt is overwhelming and debilitating, sometimes just a low simmer, but it always feels *right there*. There is never any shortage of fuel to feed the beast, so the whole mechanism is constantly nourished to administer shame and a general feeling of incompetency. Add our carefully curated social media world, which not only affects our sense of success and failure but also furnishes our children with an unprecedented brand of expectations, and boom: we are the generation that does more for our kids than ever in history yet feels the guiltiest. Virtually every one of my friends provides more than they had growing up, and still the mantra we buy into is *not enough, not enough, not enough*.

Meanwhile, if we developed the chops to tune out the ordinary complaints of children, we'd see mostly happy kids, loved and nurtured, cared for and treasured. At what point parents began accepting the disgruntlements of seventh graders as a factual State of the Union, I'm not sure, but just because they whine and fuss, or beg and plead, or even experience an actual parent letdown doesn't mean we are ruining our families and doing everything wrong. We've lost the ability to flex, to shrug off missteps, to say *I'm sorry* and move on, to prioritize the big picture while lending grace to the subplots.

My youngest asked me this week to eat lunch with her at school, and with every workday spoken for and then some, I couldn't and told her so. After conjuring the most pitiful eyes in history and sulking around the living room for half an hour, she walked up to me and said, like a martyr, "It's all right, Mom. I forgive you."

No. Nope. No, ma'am. Forgiveness is offered to someone who has wronged you, not a mother who has a job during your 11:10 a.m. lunch slot at Buda Elementary School. My work is not a sin against you, Child of Sorrow. Most moms on the entire earth work, in fact. I refused to sink into a shame spiral because I didn't grant my snowflake's particular wish, especially since we spend most of every day in the same house together.

A few years ago, that would have sent me to the prayer closet, wringing my hands yet again at how often I wound my children. I might have let that seep into my thoughts, poisoning my hope for their healthy childhoods and our future relationships. I may have immediately compiled a list of all the moms who would drop everything, rearrange an entire day to make it happen—the ones who already eat at school twice a week. I would have made up a whole story about how neglected she felt, just a piteous, tearful, walking tragedy, and she would write an essay on feeling unloved, and her teacher would read it to her colleagues and they would lament how disappointing it was when a working mom picked her career over her child.

Instead I said, "Sorry, kid. Have a great day. See you at 2:45."

And shocker: she was fine.

You guys, the kids are fine. We are fine. We need to sturdy up a bit. The definition of great parenting is not a mother who engineers every waking moment around the whims of her kids. It is not a mom who drops all else to cater to them. It is not a parent who never, for example, throws a wooden spoon against the wall or hides in her car eating crackers while her kids search everywhere for her. It doesn't include only the ones who never missed a single event or suffered an epic, catastrophic Mom Meltdown. That family doesn't even exist.

We are not playing a zero-sum game here as we raise children for twenty-five years or more. As loath as I am to compare parenting to politics (forgive me, dear ones), it's not unlike how candidates win delegates at the state level during primaries. Although it varies between parties and states, most candidates win delegates proportionally. So if they receive 65 percent of the votes, they get at least 65 percent of that state's delegates, moving them that much closer to victory. In some cases, if a competing candidate fails to receive a minimum percentage of votes in a particular state, he forfeits all his delegates to the winning front-runner, so if he only pulled 10 percent and the minimum threshold was 15, the leading candidate receives those delegates, too, and that 10 percent simply disappears from the losing candidate's numbers.

Stick with me: the hopefuls slog this out state by state, town hall meeting by town hall meeting, over months and miles and losing sweat and blood, sometimes winning, sometimes losing, but no one state makes the entire call; it is a cumulative total of more wins than losses until they've secured the majority.

Mamas, if we are winning roughly 80 percent of the votes, if the majority poll involves laughter and nurture, attention and grace, presence and patience, *we are winning*. After all, in some cases, anything less than 20 percent falls off the map entirely; it doesn't even register as counting. We may lose dramatically in, say, a certain season or specific disaster. We may rack up some negative numbers for a spell or lose ground during the preschool years or that one horrible junior year. But victory isn't compromised by individual losses; it is the result of slogging it out season by season, conversation by conversation, over months and miles of sweat and blood, and the cumulative total of more wins than losses secures the role, anchors the majority, makes the history books.

As I mentioned in *For the Love*, my goal as a mom is to be mostly good. I may hover around 70 or 80 percent success with a 20 or 30 percent failure rate, but, if that's enough to win the White House, it's enough to win any house. Somehow, miraculously, the whole ends up being greater than its parts, and I know this because I'm a historian who now assesses my own childhood through the 80 percent window. Frankly, the other 20 percent is either recalled with grace and laughter or forgotten altogether, forfeiting its delegates to the winning side, having failed to meet the minimum threshold to seriously count.

And lest you are tempted to prop up my childhood as some ideal prototype, I want you to know how wonderful but regular it actually was, hitting practically none of the benchmarks of "attentive parenting" these days.

Well, we were a middle-class family who didn't have extra anything. My parents pawned all their jewelry in 1982 so we could have Christmas presents; I don't remember my mom (or any mom) at a single field trip or class party; we moved to four different states during my childhood (including a move in precarious eighth grade); we never flew on an airplane or took a single fancy vacation; we had crappy cars that broke down once a week; my mom went back to college when we were in elementary, middle, and high school, so we ate sandwiches for two years; all of us had in-school suspension at least once; and two of us racked up zero credits the first semester of college (unless "partying" has since become a course selection). To this day, we struggle to nurture sick spouses and children because our mom was like, *Are you bleeding? Is your fever over 103? Did you puke more than once? No? Go to school.*

My point is that we were ordinary. No parent catered to our every desire; no one provided artisanal vegan soap or taught us baby sign language or created "mental stimulation centers" in our playroom (we didn't have a playroom). We moved and struggled financially and fought and failed and fended for ourselves sometimes and went to school with strep throat. And still, here we are, healthy adults who love their parents and each other, remembering childhood fondly, gratefully, tenderly. The main elements of the story were secured, and they alone lasted.

Friends, I'm challenging the metrics. I believe we can take a handful of things quite seriously as parents and take the rest less seriously, and it is all going to be okay. You are doing an amazing job. Your children know they are loved and have felt it all these years deeply, intrinsically. If we get seven out of ten things mostly right as moms, we are winning the majority, and the majority wins the race.

And when in doubt, put a few dollars back each month for their future therapy.

Mama tried.

God made
us such a
pretty world.

–Remy Hatmaker

CHAPTER 3

BEAUTY, FOOD,
FUN, AND NAPS

A couple of years ago, I traveled to Ethiopia with a nonprofit I serve, Help One Now, and a few fellow influencers. We had an audacious goal: generate monthly sponsorships for four hundred at-risk kids to prevent imminent family disruption. It was orphan prevention. Families had to meet several criteria for sponsorship: single-parent, HIV-positive, no extended family, no job. We were serving seriously vulnerable people with zero safety nets.

Adding to this heavy work, our team drove an old van six hours a day to meet all our objectives. In rural Ethiopia. The best way I can describe this experience is by comparing it to riding a wooden roller coaster built in 1925 and missing 60 percent of its parts. We were pretty sure we were going to die any minute. You couldn't even call what we were driving on actual roads. We were shaken and bounced and slammed half to death hour after hour, and this was all aided by no air conditioning. It was vehicular trauma.

This was serious, sober work, and we labored around the clock, spending long days in the field, then long nights at our laptops, banging the drum, rallying the troops. My mind was brimming with poverty statistics and crushing stories and injustices; our conversations centered around empowerment and reform. In the middle of this work, with my dirty hair and tired body and tortured mind, a text from a girlfriend back home snuck through the precarious web of Ethiopian cell coverage:

"Party at my pool next Friday! All our friends, no kids, and margaritas!"
First thought: *Privileged American life. Gross and clueless.*
Second thought: *I'm gonna get a new bathing suit for this! Yay for pool parties!*

It's so weird to live in this world. What a bizarre tension to care deeply about the refugee crisis in Syria and also about *Gilmore Girls*. It is so disorienting to fret over aged-out foster kids while saving money for a beach vacation. Is it even okay to have fun when there is so much suffering in our communities and churches and world? What does it say about us when we love things like sports, food, travel, and fashion in a world plagued with hunger and human trafficking?

Obviously, good reader, I understand the dilemma. In this very book you are holding, I seriously discuss trauma recovery and abusive churches as well as Netflix and junior football leagues. I love people. I love curry. I love God. I love coffee tables. I care about the church, and I also care about dinner. Justice and humor are equal heavy hitters for me. I live in several categories wholeheartedly, sometimes in the same hour.

In the complicated world of Christian subculture, there is an unspoken standard, a notorious goal to "win the contest." It's there, the contest. We don't say it out loud, because it sounds ludicrous spoken into the open air, but we all know about it, we feel it. The contest is a race to see who is the better Christian, and beyond the basics of behaving, extra points are awarded to people who do the hardest work with the least amount of fluff.

Obviously, top billing goes to missionaries. This is a given, the brass ring. These are the ones who went all in, the clear winners. Doesn't matter that they debunk our American notion of international work constantly, telling us they are still normal people with normal friends and sometimes they even have fun or sin. We don't believe them. They pulled the total-obedience trigger, and now they live on Winner Island with all the other missionaries. (People who don't own TVs live on the island too.)

The rest of us still living in the land of plenty are left to battle it out for the remaining prizes. We keep a close eye on each other, paying attention to who is volunteering more, sacrificing more, spending less, misbehaving less. You know we do this. Right this second, you can envision that one person nailing the standard, the one winning the contest in your estimation, the one of which you ask: "What would _____ do?" (Or more likely: "_____ would never _____.") This is the person you remember when you need to feel bad about your Christian performance.

Laughably, hysterically, people sometimes put my name in that blank. Sisters, please. Listen, if you think for a millisecond that career ministry qualifies anyone for the prize, you are mistaken. What is "career ministry" anyway? How is my "ministry" any more "ministry" than anyone else's? Regardless, the contest hits a whole 'nother level up here among us full-timers, those of us who stand on stages and do Jesus-y things for a living. Who is the *most* Christian? Who complains the least? Who posts the most Scripture references on Instagram? Who requires less downtime?

Who works harder? Who does the most good? Who is *always* happy to be alive and shows the least humanity?

Oh, trust me: the struggle is so real.

Or maybe you favor the individual events in the contest and your toughest competitor is yourself. Am I wasting my life on things that don't matter? Is God proud of me? Should I be more devout, serious, dedicated? Am I radical enough? Do I "lay down my life for others," and are all my "treasures in heaven"? Perhaps you don't look sideways for these criteria but wage a constant, discouraging war against yourself. I cannot think of a greater burden than imagining God's perpetual disappointment.

The contest is exhausting and demoralizing. And then I remember something else: it isn't even biblical. It's not how the family works. Forget for a moment the whole notion of comparing Christian obedience, which is clearly insane, a man-made competition that pits apples against oranges, kale against cheeseburgers. It's so silly and unregulated and impossible. Total nonsense, a full miscalculation of Jesus's new way of living, a game with no winners that centers on human performance over freedom in Christ. In a race to be faithful, we succumb to pride, rigging and ruining the whole thing.

But that aside, the idea that winning Christians enjoy the least number of good-and-fun things (all branded as selfish and frivolous) is a mess. These good-and-fun things run the gamut from basic merriment to time off to pretty things to outside interests not found in the New Testament. The Christian guilt that often accompanies these pursuits can be daunting, tempting us to downplay them in certain company.

The thing is, God absolutely created us and His world with tastes and sights and sounds and connections designed to thrill. He thought up humor and laughter and delicious flavors coaxed from the earth. He gave us beautiful colors and dance and music and the gift of language. He invented apples and beaches and sex and baby lambs.

In addition to an overabundance of raw materials, God designed community to connect with Him and each other through feasts and parties and wide tables set with bread and honey and wine. He fundamentally, theologically established the Sabbath, every seventh day for people and every seventh year for the land, declaring rest not just helpful but holy. God proclaimed Jubilee once every fifty years, a year of debt cancellation and universal pardon, a time for reconciliation between adversaries and a radical display of God's mercies.

In other words, God is into beauty, food, fun, and naps.

It often feels unchristian to enjoy life, especially knowing what we know and seeing what we see. Appropriately, we are deeply connected to human suffering and setting wrongs right; we care about sharing and generosity and making sure our grossest, basest selves don't overtake our character. A life spent entirely on pleasure is the emptiest of containers. We know this in our souls, in our Scriptures. God positively told us to stay close to the brokenhearted, the hungry, the hurting; that is where He is and where some of His best work is going down.

But wisdom also embraces the rest of the plan, which includes a beautiful world and beautiful people and beautiful delights *meant to be enjoyed*. When the story we tell ourselves is that God is a bit punitive and stern and we are only here to serve His bottom line and basically just suffer until we die and finally get to heaven, then it makes sense that embracing pleasure is out of bounds and only lesser Christians succumb, those disqualified for the contest.

But if we absorb the full counsel of Scripture and acknowledge that God sincerely loves us and gave us a whole world of gifts and joys, we discover many secular things we love are actually sacred. I was on Voxer with five dear girlfriends yesterday, and my beautiful friend Sarah reminded us of "the ministry of a new haircut." Oh, my stars and gardens, yes. It's like a rebirth. We made a quick list of various ministries that buoy our spirits and quicken our steps: an old pair of comfy jeans, a crisp pair of new jeans, a pedicure, Spotify, freshly cut grass, a new bra (this ministry is so real, you guys), toes in sand, chips and salsa, a career accomplishment, a really outstanding concert, chopped onions and garlic in olive oil, a fuzzy blanket, a squishy baby, a new reading chair.

This world is hard and scary, and it is also phenomenal and gorgeous and thrilling and amazing. Reader, there is a middle place, holy ground, where we learn to embrace the fasting and the feast, for both are God ordained. There is a time to press into sacrifice, restraint, self-denial, deferment. There is also a time to open wide our arms to adventure, laughter, fulfillment, gladness. A Christian in tune with God's whole character neither regards herself as too important or too unworthy to enjoy this life. Yes, we are part of God's plan to heal the world, but we are also sons and daughters in the family. We are not just the distributors of God's abundant mercies but also their recipients.

Back to Ethiopia. As I mentioned, we were working with an incredibly fragile community plagued with food insecurity, sickness, and economic collapse. These were not frivolous people with the luxury of outside interests. We lived in two entirely different worlds, one marked by privilege and one by poverty.

And yet.

Each home we visited had at least one beautiful piece of fabric hanging on the wall. Even the most humble hosts offered coffee in lovely cups. Kids, really vulnerable kids, screeched and laughed as they played soccer up and down the streets. The whole town vibrated with Ethiopian music, Teddy Afro, the national favorite, aggressive and blaring and always too loud. The town square practically sizzled with the spicy smells of berbere and tibs and doro wat.

In other words, they were also into beauty, food, fun, and music.

Of course they were.

God gave humanity many healing tools, and they exist far beyond circumstances. Some of them are traditionally spiritual: prayer, communion, sanctuary, Scripture. The sacraments have always brought us back home to God. But so many others are tactile, physical, of soil and earth, flesh and blood. Some are covert operators of grace, unlikely sources of joy, like a beautiful piece of art, a song, a perfectly told story around a dinner table, a pool party with friends and margaritas. These also count, they matter, they are to be consumed and enjoyed with gusto, despite suffering, even in the midst of suffering.

God gives us both Good News and good times, and neither cancels out the other. What a wonderful world, what a wonderful life, what a wonderful God.

I hate people who
are not *serious*
about meals.
It is so *shallow*
of them.[1]

–Oscar Wilde

CHAPTER 4

GROCERY STORE THEOLOGY

ook, I realize I put five children in this family on purpose. I did not accidentally end up with an enormous family against my will. And I also realize that this many dependents requires more of everything—more money, more work, more energy, more cell phone tracker apps (I am a laid-back mama, but I will track a phone so hard). This is part and parcel of Big Family Life, and I'm down.

The only thing I wish my multiple kids did less was eat.

Y'all, they want to eat every single day. Several times!

If you could see how much food five children and their friends go through, you would swear on a stack of Bibles they all had tapeworms. It is actually insane. They deplete my pantry by 30 percent within fifteen minutes of a grocery store run. It is like living with savage wilderness people who come across a fresh animal carcass.

This is partly why I loathe the grocery store. I realize people who love food as much as I do typically swoon over shopping, but not this home cook. I've let the fridge and pantry whittle down to half a package of rice and an old bottle of fish sauce before finally dragging my butt to the store to fend off starvation. Why is it so hard? Wasn't I just here? Are malnourished robbers breaking in at night and eating our food? It seems physically impossible these people devoured all the food I bought just one minute ago. There has to be a different explanation than simply my kids demolishing it all like champion competitive eaters.

But I also despise the grocery store because of all its horsecrappery.

I, like all reasonable and decent citizens, traverse the exact same grocery store path every trip. This is just civilized. I have a couple of friends who shop helter-skelter—different starting places, different routes, random patterns—and I've recommended them for intervention. Listen, it's a free country, so I respect your right to start with the middle aisles and end with the perimeter (*I guess*), but do the same thing every time, for the love of the land. This seems like baseline grocery store theology.

Anyhow, I begin my odyssey in produce. I immediately identify which shoppers I am now going to awkwardly encounter for the next hour. The, say, four of us have launched our journeys at the same time, and we will now follow a nearly identical path through the store. Right when you think you've broken free from the pack, one of them turns down Aisle 7 from the opposite end: *We meet again, Lady in Green.*

This is approximately one thousand times worse if it is someone I know. Because now we are required to dialogue on each passing, and what really is there to say after the first grocery store conversation?

Oh, spaghetti sauce, I see. What would we do without Prego, amirite?

Your basket is looking full! Which, I guess, makes sense. Because of the shopping.

Hey again! I don't usually buy this crap cereal. This is for a class project. (Lies.)

Criminy! How are we maintaining an identical pace through thirty thousand square feet? This is the only time I will disrupt my route, to untangle from the socially awkward prison of repetitive small talk. This is the introvert's nightmare, and I am not above dismantling my orderly system to escape another eight-second discussion on the price of wheat bread. So I skip the dairy section and go straight to paper goods this time . . . what is this, the Spanish Inquisition?

Then there is the hypocritical dance required every time I grocery shop. If you've been around me the last few years, you know I'm pretty committed to real food and whole ingredients, and I'll pay double for organic in a hot minute. Our meat is carefully sourced, and I cook almost everything from scratch. I forced my whole family to watch *Food, Inc.* and *Super Size Me*, and we listened to *Forks Over Knives* on audio on a road trip once (the Hatmakers know how to party).

So I don't know how to help you process the $6.99 box of Flavor Blasted Goldfish and coffee creamer made entirely of chemicals I purchase every.single.time. To say nothing of the Oreos and Totino's frozen pizzas. Premade, processed pudding cups? Sure. Kraft Macaroni and Cheese? We take vitamins. Not all our food comes from someone's farm, is what I'm saying. If 75 percent hails from the actual earth and 25 percent comes from a steel vat of partially hydrogenated oil in a laboratory, I'm willing to make this ideological leap. Mama's busy sometimes.

But admittedly, some items in our modern grocery stores feel like they are heralding end times. In the deli department, a wandering eye will spot such delightful foodstuffs as an "olive loaf." Surely you agree that anytime the word "loaf" is applied to a meat product, we are approaching societal breakdown. We have a brand called Steak-umm, which is a "chopped and formed emulsified meat product that is comprised of beef trimmings left over after an animal is slaughtered." These are the sorts of exported products that make the rest of the world admire America. Oh sure, Italy, you may have hand-rolled pasta from a local wheat mill and cheese made from your cousin's grass-fed cows, but we have chicken nuggets made from factory runoff meat slurry. Waste not, want not, is what we say, *Italy*. Here's a low-quality fast-food restaurant for your nation's capital. You're welcome.

Also, I've never mastered the art of meal planning (and by "art" I mean basic diligence exercised by most healthy adults). The whole idea of planning out two weeks of meals and recipes and lists makes me want to cover my eyes like a southern damsel. I mean, *I write entire books* but can't muster the discipline to compile a one-page list. It's too much work! What am I supposed to do, think about it in advance and write it all down?? Adulting is hard. So instead, I go to the grocery store and spend three times more money than necessary.

But at least five times during every trip, I recall some dinner idea and spend five minutes pulling up the recipe on my tiny phone in the middle of Aisle 4, like a rock in a river everyone has to flow around. This is immediately followed by a text to whoever is home: Can you check if we have coconut milk? Do we have any green onions left? How many ounces is the can of tomato sauce in the pantry? Is there still a jar of ghee in the back of the fridge? (Everyone loves my grocery store texts. This is how families bond.)

Finally I get to the checkout lane. Without exception, my cart is piled so dangerously high that I am holding six items in my hands and tucked into my armpits that literally could not fit, while simultaneously keeping the precarious bounty from spilling off the cart with my right foot. (One time I checked out with Sydney and Remy, who is Ethiopian, and between the different-skinned girls and ridiculous cart, the checker asked, "Do you run a children's home?" For the love.)

The intuitive bagger immediately gets a second cart, because my burgeoning basket could basically qualify for vehicular manslaughter should it ram an unsuspecting customer. It weighs around eight hundred pounds and could lay waste to a small child caught in its inertia.

Thus begins the long haul home. As I pull into the driveway, I see my children scatter like a bunch of draft dodgers during the Vietnam War. (Just in case you wondered how naturally helpful the children of a pastor and Christian author are, now you know. Zero percent.)

The unloading and putting away of the groceries is easily the worst part, and here is the singular moment those five kids come in handy. It's like a small staff. I fetch them from their hiding spots as my labor force, and they manage to eat three entire bags of food between the car and kitchen. After throwing out the old takeout containers, mysterious leftovers, and sad cilantro (why can I never use it in time?), I engage the Tetris of fridge organization and rearrange the pantry from whatever bullcrap disorder my kids inflicted, because it seems fine to them to put the lentils next to the baking powder. Then it is the rinsing of the produce, the breaking down of the cardboard for recycling, the folding of the twenty-nine reusable grocery bags, and the washing of the Tupperware resuscitated from cryopreservation.

From start to finish, this whole process takes around seventeen years.

At least I'll only have to do it again six days from now.

JEN'S GROCERY STORE DAY SUPER SANDWICH

This is my go-to recipe on shopping day, because by the time I've put the food in the basket, put the food on the conveyer belt, put the food into the car, taken the food into the house, washed the food, put the food in the fridge/freezer/pantry, I'M OVER THE FOOD. This is not a day to make an elaborate meal, because I have angry feelings toward food. So, make the grocery deli and bakery your sous chefs:

Bakery:
Ciabatta bread (one loaf for normal families, two for freakishly large families like ours)

Deli Counter:
Tub of pesto
¼ lb pepperoni
¼ lb salami
¼ lb ham
¼ lb mozzerella, sliced thin
Tub of marinara

Produce section:
Container of butter lettuce (why do the other lettuces even try?)
1–2 tomatoes
Fresh basil
Purple onions, if they won't incite mob violence
Pineapple

Preheat the oven to 350 degrees. Slice your ciabatta loaf in half lengthways. Spread a thin layer of pesto on the bottom, layer up the meats, cheese, and veggies and basil, and spread a thin layer of marinara on the top half. Close 'er up, stick on a sheet pan, cover with foil, and warm through for about fifteen minutes. Slice and serve with cute little individual bowls of marinara, because the only thing better than marinara is more marinara.

Cut up a pineapple for your "side dish," because you are still very much over all the food.

This entire procedure takes five minutes to assemble. Maddeningly, your people will fall all over themselves loving this dinner while barely commenting on the two-hour Indian feast you prepared the night before. I TOASTED AND GROUND MY OWN SPICES WHILE MAKING BIRYANI AND NAAN, and they are like, *Mmmmm! Store-bought pesto on bread! Delicious, Mom! You're a great cook!* When in fact, I've made a sandwich.

Fine. I'm awesome.

It's not the load
that *breaks* you
down; it's the way
you *carry* it.[1]

–LENA HORNE

CHAPTER 5

WE LIVE

In 2015, I had the opportunity to speak on the farewell tour of Women of Faith after its twenty years of faithful service to women. These gals, some in their sixties, seventies, and even eighties, have changed so many lives, I cannot even imagine what their corner of heaven is going to look like. (It will be very crowded with plenty of inappropriate humor, I can tell you that.)

Sandi Patty was one of the longtime WOF contributors. If you don't know Sandi, there is a zero percent chance you grew up evangelical in the eighties. I wore her tapes plumb out. She is a singing legend, and her particular flair involves super high, grand finishes. The kind where you just fall out. I adore her. I adore her to the ends of the universe, her and her whole big crazy wild family.

One weekend on the tour, she asked for prayer for an impending procedure on her vocal cords, kind of a scary one, and since I am a stable adult, I hollered:

"Not her voice, Lord! Anything but her voice! Take her legs!"

One should rethink asking me to pray for a person's needs.

I can't count how many times I've witnessed something similar: the uber healthy fitness buff contracts heart disease. The most devoted mom loses a child. The faithful wife is left behind for another woman. The committed pastor is cannibalized by his elder board. The first-rate athlete loses mobility.

The *main thing* is attacked, and no amount of devotion could stop it.

It is a watershed moment when we start bargaining with God: *Anything but this, Lord. I did everything right! I invested wholeheartedly. I sacrificed greatly. I nurtured this specifically. I need this particularly. I love this especially. How could* this *go down despite my dedication?*

Until recently, I possessed a very developed sense of entitlement to my best things. I mostly expected them to live on their own island of protection, tucked away from harm, disease, disintegration. I bought the notion that my own attentiveness and control would maintain the island, and for good measure, I imagined that God Himself endorsed my system. Especially if that particular main thing was used in His service (double immunity!). I invoked "a hedge of protection" around my island like contemporary prayer circles taught me to. I read the books with Ten Steps for _____ and recorded every lecture on Eight Ways to _____ and implemented the basic protective measures the experts recommended. I assumed the cocktail of diligence, obedience, privilege, and vigilance would insulate my best things from harm.

It was a lovely fantasy. Not biblical or sensible or rational, but lovely.

The problem is life.

Last year, within six months, I had five main things go down, catastrophically. Two of them involved my children, easily the most treasured inhabitants on the island. All illusion of control, all assumed security—vanished. The details are private, but I can tell you this: we were rattled to the foundation of this family. It was like looking down at your feet on solid ground and watching it erode as you stood there. When you believe your island has been protected under your vigilant watch, then you discover your surveillance was flawed, or you find out one of your beloved inhabitants has struggled alone mightily, it will knock you so flat you fear you'll never rise again.

It is a sobering realization that our children must live a real life in a real world, that they are targets, vulnerable to the same suffering that plagues us all. They will experience everything we never wanted for them: heartache, trauma, fear, isolation, agony, loss. They will not be the first generation to live a pain-free life. They will not be the only human beings to make it out unscathed. We can have it all in place, all in check, all under our thumb, and they are still not exempted from Jesus's statement: "In this world you will have trouble" (John 16:33). It is the most awful situation. What a horrible system.

During this same season, I noticed something strange happening with my hands. My knuckles began stiffening, my tendons started to knot, and my fingers began to draw in. Because I am very careful about my health, I completely ignored it. Sure, I had some simultaneous symptoms in my foot and shoulders, but I chalked it all up to "random weirdness" (a medical term I invented).

Finally, one evening on my porch, I asked my friends, "Do you think my hands look strange?" and held them up. Because my friend Tray is merciful, he shouted, "Gross! I can see that from here!" My friend Jenny Web-diagnosed me in four minutes with a condition called Dupuytren's contracture, and an appointment with a hand orthopedist confirmed it.

Basically, I have an irreversible, degenerative condition almost exclusively found in old men. In fact, there are four ancillary symptoms that sometimes accompany DC and I have all but one, and the only reason I do not exhibit that manifestation is because it is penis related, so there you are. The upside to this diagnosis is that my orthopedist constantly tells me how young I am. (I am the clear Prom Queen of the Waiting Room.) The downside is that there is no cure or reversal and my hands are going down.

During these exact months, my brother was swept up in a massive group injustice, an absolute nightmare that stole an entire year of peace and destroyed dozens of lives and families. It traumatized several dear friends, and had it simply been a different day, my husband and dad would've been involved too. The injustice shook us to the core, and when there was nothing left in the tank, when we were all on empty, my mom was diagnosed with cancer.

Somewhere in the midst of this season, I got mad. I went from wailing grief to fury: Really? My kids? Of all the people! How could this be? How could so much struggle have taken place under my own roof? My brother and mom? My beloveds. This is unfair and wrong and low and mean, and I am not having it. I am not. I am livid. And my hands? They aren't remotely as important as my family, but still! Now? This is how I work, God! For YOU. I am a writer, for the love of the land. I do not have space to process this physical loss right now. My family, my hands—this is the substance of my best work.

I had no idea how addicted to self-rule I was, or how much confidence I placed in false security. Stumbling around in the debris of dreams I thought I'd earned for me and mine was like being in a dark and lonely valley. I felt white-hot panic that everything was an illusion, it was all slipping, it was never even there. What else didn't I know? What else was breaking down? I thought we'd paved a yellow brick road straight into our predictable futures. I had never been so scared. I would be in a perfectly ordinary setting and feel the searing tickle of fear snake up my spine and envelope my entire head until my brain felt on fire. I didn't sleep a full night for months.

Somewhere deep within, from the place I'd deposited God's Word my entire life, finally rose a quiet truth that laid the first paver stone out of anguish: "God has not given you a spirit of fear." I do not mean this in any contrived, pithy Sunday School way. It emerged as the only solid piece of ground to stand on: fear is a liar. It cannot be relied upon to lead well, to lead out, or to lead forward. It is an untrustworthy emotion, not of God, and it never leads to health, wholeness, wisdom, or resurrection. And since fear was my primary state of mind, I knew everything I was imagining, concluding, and assuming was a lie. I wasn't yet able to envision an alternative, but simply understanding that I was constructing a false narrative was the first pump of the brakes.

Good reader, you may be in a season of suffering, too, and it may have understandably catapulted you into alarm. Or it could be that fear is your default state; you simply live in it. Some of us were raised afraid and learned to view the world through the lens of dread. (My girlfriend's mother sends us terror alerts, worrisome weather reports, and news on local criminal activity anytime we are taking a trip together. We are forty-two-year-olds.)

The Bible is so incredibly helpful because, truly, God has not given us a spirit of fear, but of power and of love and a sound mind (2 Timothy 1:7). Practically, that means making decisions out of fear, drawing conclusions from a place of fear, and getting stuck in the trappings of fear will lead us away from the truth, away from health, away from Jesus. It will, choice by choice, take us further from the sound mind and place of power God carved out for us. In short, it will mess us up. Simply identifying fear as the dominant emotion is a helpful red flag. It tells us: Whoa up, sister. These thoughts and ideas cannot be trusted.

Once I admitted to operating out of a destructive head space, I shook off a bit of paralysis and started putting into practice the spiritual disciplines I preach. First at bat: declaring faithfulness—not so much mine (as I kicked a piece of our fence down in fury) but God's. I remembered: He is good. He has always been good. He loves us, and He is here. He is paying attention, and He heals. He can redeem what has been harmed. I do believe this. I was so terrified that I forgot for a minute, but I remembered. It was such a comfort that I cried from relief. God is faithful. He can be trusted.

Next up: community. Probably the darkest days of my life were the ones between discovery and disclosure. I am a member of a small friend tribe forged by one million moments of confession, transparency, truthfulness, and vulnerability. We've fought hard and won intimacy in life's trenches together for years and years and years. Hand to God, there is not one thing unsaid among us. So I finally reached out and said:

I need you.

In the whole of my life, I will never forget sitting with our friends, crying together, praying together, their assurances of solidarity healing my heart on the spot. We pushed the fear back even more, their words of wisdom chipping through the ice of loneliness. Isolation concentrates every struggle. The longer we keep our heartaches tucked away in the dark, the more menacing they become. Pulling them into the light among trusted people who love you is, I swear, 50 percent of the recovery process.

Then: do the work. In our case, this looked like counseling, education, hard conversations (and lots of them), and speaking God's Word over our family. Healing requires partnering with Jesus in the work He is accomplishing in us. We move. We engage. We do the things. Sometimes that involves therapy or medication, and by the way, there is no shame in either. It is not "lack of faith." Rather, it is a sign of incredible strength. Whether you go for preventative maintenance or because you are hanging on by a thread, I've always believed that when Scripture describes "gifts of healing," counselors are a part of that special group. They help us heal. They give us tools. They walk us through recovery. They remind us of our hope.

There is nothing weak about being in the care of a counselor. That is strong, sister. That says you are not passively waiting for your strength, your restoration. You are doing the work, poking the bear. You are actively laboring with God and making good use of someone else's gifts to develop into a stronger, healthier person. Bravo, I say! May we use any tool possible as we pursue healthy marriages, healthy kids, and healthy souls. To abuse and suffering and loss and grief and pain and a horrible enemy, I say: *Come at us, bro.* We're not going to take this stuff lying down.

The truth is, God created us with resiliency. Mankind is incredibly able to heal, to rise back up, to stare down pain with moxie. Jesus strengthens our minds for the task of recovery. We've got chops, girls. Pain is universal; there is no avoiding it, no system that will sidestep struggle. This terrible, mean voice screams out, *"What did you do wrong? How did you go so terribly off the script?"* when life bursts at the seams, but that's a lie. Life can be hard because life can be hard. We're not doing it wrong. What matters is excavating our pluck from the rubble and refusing to be defined by loss. Sometimes it looks like fury, sometimes determination, activated by a flash of our eyes and a straightening of our spines. Rather than cower under its weight, we force pain into a partnership, using it to grow, to learn, to catapult us into a deeper, wider, sturdier life.

In our family we read, we learned, went to counseling, studied, took constant temperature checks. And then we covered it all with spoken truth. A dear mentor sent me this exact text:

No matter what is stirred up, you stay tied down. Anchored down. I see debris flying—swirling like a tornado over your head—but I see you tied by a rope around your waist that is holding your feet to the ground. I see you up on your tip toes. Flatten those feet on the ground and stand firm. Trust Jesus. Trust Him with what you cannot reconcile.

So I did that. I flattened my feet, reclaimed my moxie, and told my people:

Your future is beautiful and purposed.
You are exactly as God planned you.
Jesus loves us and is with us.
We are not fragile. We are overcomers.
Our bodies may suffer, but our spirits LIVE.

And I am here to tell you today, as I write this, *we live*. Dear ones, it was just a bit ago I thought I would never smile again. And even worse, I thought I would be scared the rest of my life. Some things I'd counted on were gone, and they left a vacuum of insecurity.

But God has not given us a spirit of fear, nor has He saddled us with a spirit of defeat. We live because Jesus lives, because He is real and present and moving and working and He will not have us conquered. This is not hoodoo; it is a powerful reality. Flatten your feet, because nothing in your life is too dead for resurrection. It can be the very worst thing, the main thing, the one thing of which you said *anything but that*. Darkness can find your soul or marriage or child or body in ways that you begged against, that you blocked in every way. It can be worse than you think and more crushing than you imagined.

And even then, *we live*. This is the power of Christ in us. Rock bottom teaches us that God is who He says He is and He can do what He says He can do. We buy what we've been selling because it is real. God's healing work means actual lives are restored, actual hearts are mended, actual strength is renewed. Real marriages can come back to life, flesh and blood families are repaired, and, miraculously, those very fractures fuse back stronger than before.

We live.

Hallelujah.

Children of the same family, the same blood, with the same first *associations* and *habits*, have some means of *enjoyment* in their *power*, which no subsequent connections can supply.[1]

–JANE AUSTEN

CHAPTER 6

PRIVATE BABY

My mom and dad had three daughters in a row, then had a surprise fourth baby they called "Product Failure" behind closed doors. I was the oldest, and Drew was born when I was nine and a half. We only had girl cousins on both sides, so the addition of a boy to such an estrogen-laden family felt like an honest-to-God miracle. My sisters and I were charmed out of our minds from the first second he took a breath.

Because he was an oopsie-daisy, Mom had given all her baby stuff away by the time he arrived. So Betty Blanchard, head of the church nursery, snuck us a round metal crib from the children's ministry, and Mom put it in the corner of my bedroom. All of a sudden, during fourth grade, I had a new roommate. Every night after Mom spent the minimally necessary five minutes to put Drew to bed (because by the fourth baby, Mama ain't going through a forty-five-minute process to get a kid to sleep—girl, bye), I'd pull him out of his crib and put him in bed with me. This was entirely unsafe—no guardrails, no pillow blockade, no concern about "tummy sleeping"—but I'd tuck him in tight next to me and curl around him and marvel at how much I loved my own private baby.

That poor boy grew up exactly like you'd imagine with three older sisters. When he was around seven, my mom asked him, "Has it been really bad being the only boy in a family of sisters?" and Drew deadpanned, "Oh, Mom. If only you knew." He had no immunity against us: we dressed him up with barrettes and makeup and paraded him around with painted nails at our command. Ladies and gentlemen, he had a favorite purse. Because he was the fourth kid and it was the eighties, Mom never really knew where he was (at some point, one becomes fatigued with parenting), so we jointly raised him, not unlike a pack of wolves.

Don't you dare feel sorry for him: he found a way to benefit from older sisters. He would "randomly" show up when we had sleepovers and pool parties, and our friends kissed and fawned over him his entire childhood. Drew had a knack for charm and exercised it shamelessly if it meant he could cozy up to my girl-friends during a movie. Joke was on him, because small-town life meant three of my best friends became his middle school health, geometry, and science teachers with memories of Drew leaning innocently against them like he had no idea those were teenage breasts under his cheek. *Yes, ma'am, Ni . . . uh, Mrs. McMullen, and please try to forget how I took pictures of you in the pool through my bedroom window five years ago.*

Let me assure any reader with a bunch of girls and one boy, especially if he is the baby—that kid will be overloved his whole life. He will have extra mothers who continue to coddle him long after it is remotely appropriate. Furthermore, they will compete for his attention as if he is the dreamy star of a Disney movie. Once, after a family gathering, my sister Lindsay called me, sincerely furious at our other sister: "I get so mad when we are all together, because Cortney hogs Drew the entire time!" Just LOL, you guys.

Brandon has forever eye-rolled me and my sisters for over-attending to Drew who is, by the letter of the law, a grown man, although he was seven years old when Brandon first walked in our door. Much like our guy friends and boyfriends always took Drew under their wings like stand-in brothers, Brandon became a true brother, as did Cortney's husband, Zac. When Drew was still in elementary school, he and Brandon would slap each other's inner wrists with two fingers, and the first one to quit lost. My sisters and I objected in horror as Drew refused to give in while tears rolled down his face. This was boy behavior we never understood, not unlike Brandon driving his car parallel to us on the highway while Drew hung his naked butt out of the window, then pulling in front of us and lobbing strawberries from their Sonic Dr. Peppers at our windshield. Never mind that one was a married adult in his twenties and the other was in middle school: they both only had sisters and were making up for lost time.

You might think two parents would object to these shenanigans, but you would be wrong. Drew had an entirely different mom and dad than I did. I had parents who enforced an 11:30 p.m. curfew until I went to college. Drew had parents who vaguely remembered him coming in at 2:30 a.m. as a high school sophomore, but they can't really recall because of all the sleep they were prioritizing. Mom and Dad disciplined me with spanking spoons, five hundred sentences ("It is always best to tell the truth . . ."), groundings, and revoked privileges, but when I mocked Drew's spring-break-teen lifestyle, Mom told me, "Groundings were difficult because it punished us." Oh my gosh. I cannot. This is the same mother who capitulated to her *twelve-year-old* son to let him drive. She protests this charge by noting that "it was only the last five miles home from church."

During our teen and college years, Lindsay and I formed the top group of siblings, and Cortney and Drew comprised the bottom team. That was the season when a six- and ten-year age gap was the most pronounced. Drew was an eighth grader the year I delivered my first son. I largely missed Drew and Cortney's teens while traversing young adulthood. Because I was so square and by-the-book and my siblings were so, um, not that, we weren't sure how to connect across personalities and life stages for a while. Lindsay was my bridge to Cortney, and Cortney was her bridge to Drew, but without them, we weren't sure how to get to each other. I continued to loosen up while they started tightening up, getting us much closer to shared middle territory, but it took a few years to give each other permission to be different grown-ups than our childhood roles dictated.

Now, in our thirties and forties, we've developed a whole new adult group including all four of us. We easily and seamlessly spend time in pairs, threes, or all together, which is so overwhelming and encompassing, it is a miracle our spouses have remained wed to us. We are quite a fortress. Our family vernacular is so concrete, Brandon can finish all our stories and predict every quote we'll repeat for the ten-thousandth time, bless him lo these twenty-three years of marriage to a King kid.

Observing the arc of our sibling relationships gives me so much hope for my own kids. There are days in this household I am convinced my children will never speak again once they move out. The fighting, the personality clashes, the different ideologies— fix it, Jesus. My headstrong teenagers tell us how to parent their siblings because they are convinced everyone else is going to hell in a handbasket. I have two cowboy-boot-wearing, deer-hunting, conservative button pushers and a Virginia Woolf–reading, vegetarian, liberal feminist. I have a relentless, literal, extroverted Ethiopian and an insatiable, sarcastic, competitive athlete who used to be an only child.

It is like living in my own personal *Real World* series.

It gives me immense comfort to recall destroying my sister's closet because she wore my Pepé jeans without asking and watching my brother go Red Rage on Lindsay for calling him "Hup Head," an invented nickname created to torment. There was a stretch of time I believed I'd absolutely never like Cortney, and Drew referred to me as "Cousin Jen" because we barely knew each other. One day, we were fighting like such psychopaths, our mom stood in the middle of the living room and screamed at the top of her lungs for ten seconds, stunning us into silence. The memory of this delights my heart as I sit here.

Listen, parents in the trenches of sibling tension like me: I'm pretty sure it's all going to work out. I suspect our kids will not be the first generation to remain in adolescence and never grow into regular adults with developed brains. My siblings and I heel-kicked each other until we were black and blue, but as adults, we moved to the same city like an invading gang and spend time together *every single week*. In pairs or as a whole, we vacation, watch football, have Sunday lunch at Mom's, go to dinner, go to concerts, go to the lake, go on trips, group text, FaceTime, make inside jokes, get each other through crises, list each other as references on our résumés because we have different last names. My siblings take my kids to ballets and come to their games. I asked Cortney if I could be in the delivery room for her first baby, and she said yes without asking Zac. We love each other and like each other, and this whole family thing stuck.

Every time I read how Jesus described the kingdom as a seed or yeast, I think of parenthood. That seed is planted, that yeast is mixed in, but, my gosh, you cannot see anything happening for a while. So much investment in our kids involves delayed gratification. Is it working? Did it take? Will it ever produce anything good? Because for a bit, all you can see is hard soil with nary an inch of green growth; at first, that dough is just sitting there without a hint of rise. We know we planted, we know we included the right ingredients, but the result is invisible, hidden, terrifyingly absent. We did the work, we said the words, and now we are waiting.

Family is far more resilient than I ever hoped. I bought the lie of hyper-controlled parenting for a while, but all it produced was despair every time my kids fought or went off the script. What was I doing wrong? How could I get this back on the rails? But the thing is, family is a messy business, especially in the building years. This is true for literally every family I know, regardless if they are sweet or spicy. No exceptions. When we sow seeds of love into our children, between our children, it will eventually bear fruit. Our job is just to plant, plant, plant, and wait.

The waiting eventually paid off for our long-suffering mom. We quit fighting and sneaking out and driving her Jeep into the river (Drew), and we grew up into best friends. Of course, some things remain the same: Drew and his wife were recently house hunting, and Cortney and I kept sending listings in each of our neighborhoods with corresponding propaganda. We were still vying for his proximity, but good news, reader: they bought a house three streets over, because, after all, he was *my* private baby.

How To
(Part One)

Dear reader, maybe you, like me, find yourself often in need of instruction. *How do I get Pandora to play out of my television set? How do I keep my texts from popping up on the screen for my nosy children to read? How do I color my own hair without looking like Liza Minnelli?* What I'm suggesting is that life is complicated and we need someone to help us. We need tutorials. We need mentorship. We need guidance down life's thorny paths.

Well, I am here, a trustworthy advisor if ever there was one, amirite? I've identified a few sticky issues, tasks, and processes that bog us down and make our brains sad. How exactly do we do these things? How do we proceed? Are there rules or steps that might help us through hard things?

Why yes, yes there are. You are in luck today, girl. The following are entirely reasonable how-tos born out of actual life. These are tried and tested, and the results are guaranteed. (I wrote these in conjunction with my hilarious Facebook tribe, and many apologies to the overt liberties I took with your tutorials. My writing mantra is this: Any shared material is mine to butcher, narrate, embellish, or make inappropriate. It is truly hard to be my friend.)

How to go on a diet: The "sleeving" method

- *Breakfast:* egg white and veggie omelet
- *Lunch:* kale salad with 2-ounce chicken breast, assorted veggies, dressing on the side
- *Snack:* 1/2 cup of plain Greek yogurt with berries
- *Dinner:* 4 pieces of deep dish pizza, leftover mashed potatoes, chips and guac, 2 granola bars, and a sleeve of Thin Mints dunked in a mocha
- *Late snack:* another sleeve of Thin Mints and a glass of wine
- *Pre-bed final snack:* shame and regret

How to plan a family

1. Tell everyone you meet that you only want two children spaced over four years.
2. Actually have two kids in two years, because unprotected sex makes people pregnant. Feel confident that you are done.
3. Share a firm handshake with your spouse. Have a third baby. Sell all baby items in a yard sale, because obviously.
4. Make out with your spouse. Have twins, making your child count five in five years.
5. Send husband to urologist for vasectomy, because your body has done all it is going to do here and if he even shares a meaningful glance with you, you're going to have triplets.

How to wake your children up peacefully from nap time

1. Tiptoe into your own bedroom. Make absolutely no sound at all.
2. Ever so carefully climb into bed and assume a reclining position.
3. Close your eyes.

Programming Note: Your children should be fully awake by now and asking for snacks, but here is an extra step should you need it: Proceed with steps one to three above. Let yourself drift off for approximately ten to thirteen seconds but no more than fifteen. This should work without fail.

How to shop at Target

1. Make a list of two items: cotton balls and trash can. These are the only things you need.
2. Get sidetracked by the Dollar Spot, and add fifty dollars worth of items that are "only" a dollar. It is all crap, but cheap crap, and you are thrifty. You are actually saving money. (File that tidbit away to tell husband later.)
3. Rush past the clothing. Double back for the cute shirt/sweater/yoga pants facing the aisle. No need to try on. If it doesn't fit, you can put it in your trunk to return never.
4. Decide you need new shoes to go with your new shirt, even though your old lady feet can't handle cheap shoes anymore. Pick up shoe inserts to cushion the plastic. This is self-care. You are caring for your body like the Bible said to.
5. Head back toward kitchenware for trash can, and put two big

frames in your basket en route because you just remembered you wanted to attempt a feature wall in your living room like you saw on Pinterest. Also grab those storage bins because you were going to get organized this year.

6. Get trash can and also placemats, because organized people have nice table settings.

7. Head to toiletries to get cotton balls. Smell all the shampoo in the organic, natural section, and put a twelve-dollar lotion in your cart. Discover experimental face cream made of spun elfin dreams. Costs thirty-nine dollars, but your crow's-feet are making you look like Robert De Niro and this hurts your feelings.

8. Decide you need all the stuff to organize your desk. Better pens will make you smarter and more efficient.

9. Proceed to checkout, where you pay the one hundred dollars (plus) cover charge Target insists on inflicting every.single.time.

10. Grab a Starbucks or Icee for having some self-control (because you didn't buy the themed Christmas dishes), and head to the car.

11. Realize you forgot the cotton balls. Obviously.

How to organize a book club

1. Select a book.
2. Purchase said book with real dollars.
3. Place book on bedside table for the next three to four weeks.
4. Look at book each night with good intentions. If intentions could read a book, you would have read 1,248 books this year. Feel proud of your intentions. They mean so well.
5. Start book in bed and immediately fall asleep. Your intentions are genuine but they are very tired.

6. Carry book around in your purse in case you can spontaneously read somewhere, sometime, somehow. (You can't, you won't, but now your purse is denting your shoulder between the heavy book and all the other mysterious and sometimes unidentified crap you cart around. What is even in your purse? Why does it all have a thin layer of filth on it? Why is your purse a Grime Generator?)

7. Ten minutes before the guests arrive, flip through the chapters to learn the main characters' names. Try to determine if it was set in modern-day Florida or 1922 Paris. Make a quick call: Is it fiction? Read the last page. Have a sense of conclusion in case someone died or came back to life or married the best friend.

8. Serve enough wine in hopes no one will realize you didn't open the book.

9. Discover that three out of twelve girls read the whole book. Admit that "Book Club" is an excuse for women to leave their homes with impunity ("For literature! Hello!") and basically drink wine and eat snacks and talk about boobs and trash television.

Programming Note: Do not disclose step 9 to husband. Maintain position that Book Club is about nourishing your minds with well-constructed prose. What actually happens in Book Club stays in Book Club.

HOW TO GET IN BIBLE STUDY TIME

1. Send your darling children to school, grab a great cup of coffee, your Bible, notebook, and pen, and settle in at the kitchen table.

2. Bow your head in prayer to open your heart to the Word of the Lord. Get really serious and slightly emotional, because Jesus loves you and also God plus the Holy Spirit.
3. Open your eyes to find your hubby buck naked strutting across the dining room on his day off, because this was obviously the right moment for sexy time. I believe it's deep in Song of Songs: "He shall strut himself like a mighty steed across thy gaze . . ."
4. Apologize to God. (Don't worry about Jesus; He was never married. He wouldn't understand.)

How to lose baby weight: DIY/no-gym method

1. Tell yourself you can do it. Look how great you were at *gaining* the weight! Positive affirmation is important here.
2. Load baby into stroller and set off for epic one-mile walk or jog.
3. Walk or jog for what feels like eight miles. Discover it is two-thirds of one.
4. Lift five-gallon tub of laundry soap as "weights." Do five sit-ups. See? Who needs a gym? You are so motivated and thrifty. You are a Proverbs 31 woman.
5. Feel your muscles cramping and spazzing. Self-medicate with a bowl of potato salad and a side of Doritos, because you can double down on your carbs if you want to. They are in the food pyramid.
6. Decide you're okay with being chubby. Feel philosophical about this. Society doesn't get to tell you how to look. You'll intentionally keep these pounds on because you are NOT GOVERNED BY THE MAN.
7. Pour glass of wine.

8. Brag about exercise to husband. Oversell the distance/
   weight/duration/reps.
9. Vow to never do any of it again.

How to ruin your toddler's life

1. Pour him one-eighth of an inch less milk than his brother in a
   see-through cup.

Programming Note: If this doesn't work, accidentally break his
cookie in half as you lift it off the cookie sheet. Because broken
cookies don't taste the same! If these fail, give him the wrong
kind of cheese or socks with weird seams. This should effectively
destroy his happiness.

How to ruin your teenager's life

1. Breathe.
2. Don't buy her a car even though she really wants one but
   forgot to save any of her money like you told her to four
   years ago. (You could stop effectively at this step, but continue
   through the manual if teen resentment wears off.)
3. Say no to Senior Skip Day, even when he has proof, and even
   when that proof is a screenshot of an iPhone note typed up
   and shared by someone named *hottiexoxo* with instructions to
   spread the word "on the low." Your teen cannot understand
   your problem with *hottiexoxo*. You are the "most paranoid
   mom ever."
4. Keep breathing. This assaults the teen psyche more than you
   might imagine.

5. Give advice on a problem teen is having. Realize you know nothing, understand nothing, have nothing to offer, have no experience, no clue, and no chill. You're just an old lady who makes dinner.

6. Smile anyway and toast the hubs for making it this far, and dream about all the places you'll go when the nest is empty.

HOW TO GET YOUR HUSBAND TO FIX THAT THING HE'S BEEN SAYING FOR THREE MONTHS THAT HE'D FIX

1. Tell him it's fine if he doesn't know how to fix it.
2. Watch him fix it.

Programming Note: If this tried-and-true method fails, start getting estimates from professionals. As a last resort, start the project yourself. Even just pick up a hammer and walk in the general direction of the broken thing. This should effectively catapult your husband off the couch and into disgruntled service: *"I said I would do it!"*

HOW TO HELP YOUR MIDDLE SCHOOLER WITH MATH HOMEWORK

1. Have your child go to the kitchen table and set out her homework.
2. Slip up to the bathroom. Look in the mirror and say, "I got this. Eighth-grade geometry is not my bully."
3. Take several deep breaths like you learned while pregnant

with this child in Lamaze class, because geometry may not be your bully but your eighth-grade daughter definitely is.

4. Calmly approach the kitchen table and sit with your child. Smile. Do not spook the middle schooler. Do not make any sudden movements. Say breezily, "So what are you working on?" (Knowing full well you are about thirty-five minutes from doing the worksheet yourself, because, God love her, this girl just can't do math.)

5. Spend the next thirty-four minutes trying to explain the worksheets while mentally compiling a list of future jobs that don't require math skills.

6. At minute thirty-five, let your frazzled, despondent child get some ice cream while you rewrite some of her answers so she will at least get a C-.

7. Math homework done!

Programming Note: If you are equally confused about the geometry homework, outsource to Dad, big brother or sister (bribe with cash), smart neighbor, Grandma or Grandpa, before-school tutoring, YouTube, or Google. You are good at other things. Continue to feel good about self.

How to go swimsuit shopping three months postpartum

1. Gather as many "figure-flattering" swimsuits as possible.

2. Hastily try them on. Look in the mirror, but only through squinted eyes to soften the blow. Wear sunglasses if this helps.

3. Realize the form-fitting material reveals every lump and bump you received as parting gifts from your pregnancy. Have confused feelings about the underside of your butt. What

exactly has happened back there? Something has gone wrong. Some stuff is out of place.

4. Put all the swimsuits back.
5. Weep a little.
6. Eat some Cadbury mini eggs.
7. Wear an old suit to the pool, because you deserve that water even though your nipples are still the size of silver dollar pancakes and your belly skin is like Laffy Taffy. Whatever, haters ("haters" being the swimsuits). Your body gave birth to a *human being*, and if it wants to go to the pool, it will go in all its glory.

Programming Note: If sanity is important to you, simply execute steps 6 and 7 and be done with it.

Home is
the *nicest*
word there is.[1]

–Laura Ingalls Wilder

CHAPTER 7

IT'S JUST PAINT

Maybe the most absurd day of my life was getting an e-mail from an executive at HGTV asking if I would consider developing a show around our family. Y'all, I *howled*. What in the actual? Mind you, the catalyst for this proposition was a blog I wrote about being a very, very, incredibly terrible end-of-school mom, which landed me on *The Today Show* for a scant four-minute segment in which, trying to appear breezy, I miscalculated the height of the chair and air-leaned on the arm with my elbow. Delightfully, I also wasn't wearing panties, because I usually manage eight out of every ten given details and packing underwear missed the cut. It is very hard to do everything expected of adulthood, and I appreciate your understanding. But back to HGTV.

My mediocrity was finally paying off!

After sending in a very professional video, which my then fifteen-year-old captured on his iPhone, we found ourselves filming a "sizzle" a mere two weeks later (I will set fancy TV words in quotes so we can build our insider vernacular). After being dubbed "the sound bite queen" because of my fluency in sarcasm, the sizzle passed muster, a whole production crew moved to Austin, and we bought a 1908 farmhouse and set out to renovate it during eight episodes of an original show called *My Big Family Renovation.*

Obviously, this was the moment I hired a trainer and stopped eating. Do not come at me with "girl power" or "be confident in the body you have" or some such nonsense. If you would like to star in eight hours of high-definition national television content in the body you have, be my guest, gentle reader. But I was unprepared to display my muffin top and FUA (Flabby Upper Arms) on the network of homes and gardens next to their other teeny little hosts and "talent." No thank you, sirs. I didn't want to be "that chubby one who has a million kids and thinks she's funny." Motivating factors in finally dropping ten pounds: health, life longevity, energy level, strength? Meh. A simple case of extreme vanity on television? Get me my dumbbells.

Our living arrangements during the renovation were dismal enough to bring even Laura Bush to paint the universe with expletives. Brandon and I lived in a room off the garage, our three boys lived in a filthy camper in the backyard, and the two girls stayed in whatever room in the house wasn't under construction. Of course, the house had no electricity, no heat, and no power, and we started filming in October during what turned out to be the coldest winter in memory. A subscriber to homemade organic food, I fed my children Pop-Tarts every solitary morning for four straight months, which obviously contributed to my general feeling of well-being and competency. We had nowhere to cook, nowhere to be, nowhere to sit down, and one shower. We were dirty, cold, malnourished people who smelled like sawdust and hunger.

I am frequently asked how Brandon and I managed to renovate an entire house in these conditions for six months without
forfeiting our marriage, and my answer is simple: If you are
interested in tackling a major construction project with your
spouse, I suggest you do it on HGTV. Do you know what forces
you to behave? Cameras. GoPros. Producers. Microphones. It's
like magic! You decide not to act like a lunatic and instead appear
patient and lovely and not at all over it at 11:22 p.m. when you
are still filming that day's "reveal." You smile sweetly at your
spouse instead of, for example, barking your actual feelings
like, *"Do I look like I want to strip another room of popcorn ceilings?
Does my face communicate that this is a thing I want to include in my
life plan?"*

Nope. On camera, you are darling, witty, patient. Your children are not getting on your last blessed nerve while they "help
paint" (make it stop). You haven't been able to feel your frozen
feet for twenty-three straight days, but you are easygoing about it
because you are precious. Your "OTFs" to camera ("on the flies,"
which we sometimes called WTFs because we need a savior) are
smiley, relaxed: "Today we hit a bit of a snag with the plumb-
ing, but we've called in the experts and hope to be back on track
in no time!" That is on camera; the cursing and despair is off.
While mic'd, your husband never once yells, "You are acting like
the Blair Witch!" and instead says, "We'll figure it out, babe." In
other words, we filmed a fictional rom-com, and we hope you
enjoyed our show.

I'll tell you what we loved: our crew. We spent more time
with our producers and camera guys during those few months
than with our own flesh and blood. It was incredibly refreshing
to be outside of church work and ministry in a completely new
space with people we grew to adore. We ate lunch around the

table together every single day, and our conversations ran the gamut from our sound tech saying, "God seems like a real ass" to our cameraman Christopher confessing, "I cried so hard during *The Pursuit of Happyness* I had to leave the theater." We had so many raw and interesting and truthful discussions, but we mostly laughed every day, all day. They adored our kids, took fantastic care of us, showed up positive and hilarious daily, and I cried my ever-loving eyes out during our "wrap party" as I tried to tell them what they'd meant to our family.

And now we get to live in this quirky, charming, lovely old farmhouse, and it is everything we ever dreamed of. I've come to realize exactly what the show was: a gift. That's it, plain and simple. It was a gift to our marriage, our season of life, and our family. It has since been the scene of incalculable memories, gatherings, parties, and get-togethers. We've hosted three hundred women who helped launch my last book, nearly four hundred partners in our nonprofit (The Legacy Collective), backyard concerts, crawfish boils, Hays High School Varsity soccer team dinners, "Dinner for 10" through our church, a dozen supper clubs, ten thousand football watch parties, Halloween bashes, Christmas mornings, New Year's brunches, church partner classes, Little League football parties, friends' birthdays, Sweet Sixteen celebrations. It has been a joy and delight to throw open the doors of our old house and welcome in our neighbors and friends, our church and family.

There is nothing more meaningful, life-giving, or lovely than *home*.

Dear one, may I say something? It is not shallow or empty or frivolous to create a beautiful space to live in. It's not silly, not vainglorious, not a waste of time and energy. It doesn't make you superficial nor slide you down the godly scale. We spend the majority of our hours in our homes with our people. Creating beauty and nurture under your roof with colors that soothe, art that inspires, furniture that invites, and textures that thrill is a wonderful use of your small space on the planet.

I do not mean this in a trite, cliché way in the slightest: How could we imagine that a God who created wildflowers and waterfalls and pine trees and hummingbirds and warm sand and mountain ranges and tulips thinks beauty is nonsense? He made a gorgeous, over-the-top earth wild with colors and textures and breathtaking landscapes. And He loved it. He said it was good, so good. He made it for our pleasure as a testament to His character. He created a sensual, aesthetic, jaw-dropping world and asked us to enjoy it. If God decided to make his whole earth pretty, we can choose to make our little homes pretty without tension, guilt, or shame.

That's when the fun starts! Design and decorating, making a house a home; this is supposed to be invigorating, not paralyzing. Let's be very honest: we are not curing cancer here. As much as we shouldn't undervalue beauty, we shouldn't overthink it either. If your living room wall has the same five paint sample patches you "tested" there four years ago, you may be taking this too seriously. This is my motto when it comes to creating lovely spaces:

It's just paint.

I use that for all things. "It's just paint" also means: it's just a stain, it's just a finish, it's just a bedspread, it's just a print, it's just a couch, it's just a table, it's just an old dresser, it's just tile, it's just hardware. Seriously, the consequences here are negligible. Don't like the pulls you chose for your cabinets? Take them off and return them. There, I solved it. There is no such thing as a design emergency. There is no such thing as a decorating catastrophe. It's just paint.

Once you lift the shroud of gravity, creating a beautiful

home is fun. Like my friend Myquillyn Smith says in her book *The Nesting Place*, "It doesn't have to be perfect to be beautiful." Find colors and styles that make you feel alive and inspired and at home, and pull the trigger. Start small, start anywhere, start with one room, one corner, one piece. You want to try a funky feature wall? Grab a hammer. Want to give an old dresser a good sanding and a fresh coat of turquoise paint? Get a brush. Do your friends love neutral colors but you love red? "Currant Red" by Benjamin Moore will make your heart sing. If not a whole wall, an old chair, a console, a chandelier, a coffee table. It's just paint.

Go with what you love, not necessarily what you see on design shows or in your neighbor's house. Pay attention to what grabs *your* eye and what you are consistently drawn toward. My style is random and possibly invented: I favor a bit of "old barn" crossbred with some industrial elements, super mismatched furniture, cluttered oversized wall features, and enough color to make Joanna Gaines cry all the tears in Waco. I prefer mostly old things but some new, and I like everything to feel cozy, overstuffed, textured, warm. I want to tuck my friends into my comfy too-big-for-the-room sectional with mugs of coffee and cover their laps with crocheted blankets while I play Johnny Cash on my old record player. Somehow that sentence explains my design style.

You do *you* here. There are no rules. I used to believe there were, that you could pick only one style, one direction, and all the ancillary design elements were in subjugation. I thought vibrant could never pair with neutral, cottage could never mix with contemporary, and if it wouldn't be professionally grouped in a furniture store, it was not allowed.

But that is nonsense. If you like a bit of traditional, pops of rustic, and this one show-stopping midcentury modern piece, girl, do that thing. My favorite rooms are those that feel *collected*, not purchased all at once as a matchy, matchy package. That old lantern you found at a flea market and painted green? Hang that bad boy over your dining room table. That gorgeous vintage wallpaper you hung on one wall? I've fainted. A beautiful, textural cowhide rug under your super-modern coffee table? Yes, yes, yes, all day long. I painted some old deer horns turquoise and hung them inside an empty frame; my end tables are an old tree stump and an antique wire chicken basket, because *I am the boss of my own house.* The only rule is that you love it and it makes you happy when you look at it. That is the only guideline to obey.

None of this has to be expensive or fancy. There is no end to what you can create out of what you already have, what you thrift, what you reclaim, what you pull out of someone's dumpster or off the side of the road (I have done these exact creepy things). Paint is cheap and changes everything from an end table to kitchen cabinets to an entire room. Make an informal co-op of fifteen friends and swap furniture; one girl's tired headboard is another girl's treasure. Craigslist has pages of stuff for free or next to nothing if you'll just go haul it off. And don't forget the age-old trick of simply rearranging a room, which will cost you nothing except some grunt work and between two and six arguments with your husband.

And let this be said: the biggest waste of nonrefundable years is closing your home to guests because it is not "pretty enough" (could also insert: big enough, new enough, clean enough, stylish enough, good enough). Let me address any possible objection about my ability to open my house with confidence because it was professionally renovated: Brandon and I have piled people into every home we've ever lived in, including apartments, duplexes, tract homes jammed with little kid crap, one home with no downstairs bathroom, one home with no insulation or dishwasher, two homes with no central air, and a dozen homes still stocked with our parents' old furniture. If we delayed hospitality until we had a fully decorated home, we would have made our first friends two years ago. And even now, our old house is little and only a few folks can fit inside, so we basically spend all our friend time in the yard sitting in eleven-dollar chairs from Academy Sports + Outdoor.

Making your home pretty is nice, but making it nourishing is holy. Sister, paint that chair or hang that mirror, sure, but for the love, don't wait until everything is done before putting on a pot of chili and inviting new friends over for football. Your neighbor wants to belong far more than she wants to be impressed. Some of my favorite memories involve walking into a girlfriend's messy house, stepping over the mountain of shoes in her entryway, accepting a glass of Pinot in a plastic Mardi Gras cup, and grabbing a knife to help chop carrots. It isn't the picture-perfect feature wall that makes me want to come back; it is the friendship, the warmth, the easy welcome, the laughter.

Home is the scene of so much love and happiness, community and pot roasts. It is where you invite people in and say, "You are so welcome in this place." It is the reel our children will replay in memory the leather chair you read in, the farmhouse table you shared, the braided rug where you played eleventy-billion games of Chutes and Ladders. It is your little corner of earth, entirely yours to make lovely. In a world increasingly dominated by fear and violence and isolation and loneliness, you can claim *restoration* under your small roof, where people are nurtured and loved and fed and embraced, where God reigns and hope is spoken, and where everything from the walls to your books to the conversations communicate the sentiment penned by Julian of Norwich in the fourteenth century:

"All shall be well, and all shall be well, and all manner of thing shall be well."

Women *love* always:
when *earth* slips
from them, they take
refuge in *heaven*.[1]

–GEORGE SAND

CHAPTER 8

NO STRINGS ATTACHED

So I was the exact eighties Baptist youth group girl you think I was. If you didn't grow up in Christian subculture back then, all I can say is that we teens graduated from True Love Waits, jammed to Petra ("a wholesome alternative to Def Leppard!"), aggressively highlighted our Life Application Bibles to impress our seatmates at church, and wore T-shirts that said: "If Bo don't know Jesus, then Bo don't know Diddley," because appropriating current pop culture for Jesus Jukes seemed like an effective evangelical strategy, God bless and keep us.

I was oh so earnest. I carried my Bible to class after our youth camp pastor challenged us to, making the side-eye comment that "most of you will give up by October." Well, listen, buddy, you don't throw down the devotion gauntlet in a room full of teen Pharisees, then walk away casually. I'll see your October and raise you a fifteen-pound study Bible displayed on my desk corner in May. *How did I have any friends?*

As a firm member of the purity and holiness culture, I harbored so much judgment toward my peers. I looked down my nose at all their shenanigans and was prepared at any time, like 1 Peter 3:15 instructed, as if I was defending my senior thesis, to "give an answer for this hope I professed" (while conveniently overlooking the next sentence: "But do this with gentleness and respect"). I didn't know about that gentleness thing, but I did indeed *have answers*. Come at me, bro.

Looking back, trying to identify the motivation for my spiritual posture is tricky. What exactly compels a sixteen-year-old to isolate her classmates and peddle spiritual shame? Myriad cultural factors affected my generation of youth groupers, but it isn't the whole truth to simply cast blame on our leaders and shrug off the weird stuff we all bought into. Nor is the chief culprit my type A personality with a heavy moral compass, although those qualities contributed.

I think I was afraid.

I was scared, first and foremost, of God. What a terrifying God I crafted back then: punitive, picky, arbitrary, angry. Holiness culture meant you were always one careless French kiss away from divine disapproval, because, like Jesus said, why buy the cow when you're giving the milk away under the bleachers? I spent all my spiritual energy trying to stay on God's Good Side, which I managed around twenty-three minutes a day. It was exhausting and scary and impossible. I was petrified of God. I don't remember what I thought of Jesus. Jesus was the Side Guy.

I was also scared to love people. What if they were wrong? Wrong about what, you ask? Oh, just anything. Wrong living, wrong ideas, wrong faith, wrong crowd. If I loved someone "wrong," then I was complicit. I was lending approval to wrongness, and that would banish me from God's Good Side, obviously. Plus, I couldn't bear the disapproval of my fellow youth group pals. Any wrongness infiltrating the camp was forbidden. As warned, it starts with one wrong friend, and the next thing you know, you are a backslidden Christian at a raucous teen beer party with no opportunity to rededicate your life until next summer's youth camp.

I thought God's plan for human beings essentially involved stringent rules to help us be really good (secured by guilt—His way of keeping order), suffering and sacrifice to keep us humble, clear moral boundaries to protect our "set apartness," and a life of restraint until we could mercifully die and go to heaven. I assumed our main responsibility to other people was to point out their errors so they could repent and get with the plan.

Imagine my shock when I discovered God's *actual* plan.

As it turns out, it's a good plan (*good* meaning actually good here): send Jesus to change all the rules and set people free in every way (apparently Jesus was more than just the Side Guy!). By word and deed, example and instruction, Jesus would teach His followers to love the outcast and the poor, to embrace their communities and each other. He would give them distinct marching orders—generosity, humility, grace, inclusion, courage—and tell them it all boils down to two things: loving God and people. (He'd make this part super clear by saying it to religious leaders!) The plan had Jesus go on and on about what it means to be blessed in this life, making sure He included the upside-down stuff: meekness, mourning, community, simplicity, kindness. He gave honor to a bunch of folks in the right head space, like kids and widows and outsiders. He slayed at parties and dinners. Oh! And Jesus forgave His enemies while He was hanging on the cross, just to be clear about how forgiveness worked pragmatically.

God's plan was smart, because obviously this sort of life would change people so dramatically and permanently, they would choose to live it out in their neighborhoods and cities and countries all around the world. They wouldn't be able to help it. It's too good, this good news. It would deliver them from their prisons and fix their souls and mend the fragile places and give them a new song. This hurting, lonely world would be drawn to these people and their Savior who gave them these ideas, because who wouldn't be? Who isn't looking for grace and belonging? Everyone wants to be loved and God loves everyone, so this was the very definition of a win-win.

Such a good plan, this gospel.

The redeemed would tell this love story with their lives because they've been told over and over that love is supreme, the most excellent way, the language of their tribe, the way of their God. They'll know for sure to default to love. At least that part will remain clear through seismic changes across centuries and cultures.

This beautiful way to live seems obvious to me now, but for a couple of decades, fear kept me locked into the tidier terrain of religion and distanced from the wide-open spaces of grace. When I recall the story of God I told with my life—one of behavior and shame and elitism—I can only beg Jesus to redeem any confusion I created, stealing hope and belonging right out of the hands of people who needed it. I missed it, and consequently I caused others to miss it because no one wanted the story I was selling. I didn't even want it.

If understood, believed, and lived out, God's plan would naturally place Christians at the epicenter of their communities, like hope magnets, like soft places to fall, like living sanctuaries. We'd be coveted neighbors and trusted advocates, friends to all and enemies of none. Our reputation would precede us, and we would be such a joy to the world.

And often we deeply are. Without question, some of the bravest folks I know doing the hardest work in the darkest places with the loneliest people do so in the name of Jesus. If all Christian organizations and churches and individuals pulled up anchor, the ripple effect would reverberate to the ends of the earth. Millions of the marginalized would lose their advocates, victims would lose their defenders, hurting neighbors would lose their friends. An enormous amount of hope would vanish.

In many cases, our reputation precedes us and it is good.

But sometimes it's not.

People are famously tone deaf regarding their own clans, so a good temperature check is to ask folks outside the faith community what *they* see. We should expect the same benchmarks Paul gave the early church: love, joy, peace, patience, kindness, goodness, faithfulness, gentleness, and self-control. (I sang it in my head. Cannot be helped. Thanks, Vacation Bible School circa 1981.) This observation would indicate the plan is in solid motion and a bunch of stuff is going right.

But when a watching world concludes the opposite, fundamentally, deeply at faith's core, something has gone dreadfully off the rails. For a minute, let's push issues and controversy and legislation and talking points aside. What does it mean when our communities construe Christians as mean, judgmental, hypocritical, and exclusive? What does it reveal? Something along the chain of command has broken down terribly. God did not order the Code Red, so we should not have this much blood on our hands. ("God, were you clear about the love thing?" "Crystal.")

Is it because Christ-followers have famously preferred the fruits of the mind over the fruits of the Spirit? Do we cling too tightly to dogma and too loosely to love? When Being Right is our highest aim, our most intimate bedfellows are academics, apologetics, and rigorous defense, and we have to use the tools of the world to secure our rank. Within this paradigm, it is easy to believe God's pleasure in us hinges on our aggressive defense of the kingdom, when, in fact, He told us repeatedly our chief identifier is how we love. (God managed to stay on His throne all these millennia, so I suspect He will not fall out of the sky on our watch.)

Or does this perception of Christians persist because we so greatly struggle to receive our own grace that we are unable to disperse it? It is difficult for human beings to accept unearned mercy. It flies in the face of our merit-based system. We want to earn our goodwill; therefore, we want others to earn theirs. But grace is an inside job first. God's love compels us to do likewise, but it must first win a hearing in our own souls if it has any chance at an outward expression. Loved people love people. Forgiven people forgive people. Adored people adore people. Freed people free people. But when we are still locked in our own prisons, it is impossible to crave the liberation of others. Misery prefers company.

Or maybe it is because we sincerely, honestly, deeply want to please God, and this world confuses and scares us because it is so far away from the promised land. So in our worry and devotion, we lash out, hoping to reclaim what has been lost. We crave spiritual territory in dark places, but that desire presents as narrowness and anger and fear. I identify with this instinct so deeply. It is a complicated dance, and we easily confuse our place in the narrative. Desperately wanting God's kingdom to come, we lead with the law, like a sixteen-year-old girl who thought a Bible on a desk corner would represent the story of God more than the warm, safe embrace of human connection.

But the law was never sufficient to make all things new. That is precisely why Jesus came. The law fell short for personal piety, societal restoration, and rightness with God. It didn't build bridges toward salvation or set people free. It only made folks feel small and inept, outsiders to an ideology that proved impossible.

The law was a heavy yoke upon tired necks, and people buckled under its weight.

Which is why the law of love introduced by Jesus is the story to tell.

It is the story that saves and heals, that invites and refuses to condemn. Christian, it is the right way and the best way. Jesus's brother James told us: *"If you really keep the royal law found in Scripture, 'Love your neighbor as yourself,' you are doing right."* We can stand rightly before God when love leads and compels us. We need not fear that He will say, "You loved too greatly, too liberally, too generously, too shockingly." The entire story of God reveals a vast, encompassing campaign to love humanity all the way home. It is the clearest picture of Jesus, who we should desire in every heart. People may hate us because of Jesus, but they should never hate Jesus because of us. The way we treat others should lead them to only one conclusion: "If this is how Jesus loves, then I'm in."

When in doubt, ask yourself: What would love feel like here, to this person? And for the sake of clarity, let's assume we are not dealing with violent or harmful behavior where someone is endangering herself or others. That is a different category of communication, so don't let a straw man keep you from engaging in *this* discussion. Which is: What does love look like in the ordinary connection between two human people? Usually it means prioritizing someone's dignity, belovedness, and experience over being right or pointing out errors. We may even discover we weren't so right after all, or at any rate, we didn't fully understand.

I've learned this deeply from friends and leaders in the black community. Previously unaware of systemic injustice, my implicit bias, and my knee-jerk reaction to black pain or outrage, I've since discovered that "Yeah, but . . ." or "Well, *I'm* not . . ." or "Okay, but what about . . ." or "No, it didn't . . ." is the opposite of love. Love means saying to someone else's story or pain or anger or experience: "I'm listening. Tell me more." Love refuses to deny or dismantle another's perspective simply because I don't share it. At its core, love means caring more about that person's soul than anything else. The New Testament coined it with a lovely phrase: *preferring others*. It's a super simple approach that would change the whole world.

My girlfriend Jessica and I were talking about the lost art of dialogue this week: the free flow of meaning between two or more people. When we are skilled at dialogue, we create safe spaces for everyone to add their own meanings to a shared pool of understanding, and no matter how much we believe differently, our perspective only occupies a bit of the pool. This may feel threatening at first, especially if the dialogue is controversial or shared between people with different beliefs. But even if we disagree, perhaps even strongly, it is still possible to hold a civil dialogue where ideas find their way out into the open.

Why is this so hard? Staying reasonable and measured and respectful in the midst of charged conversations is a lost art. The way of our generation is outrage, offense, and polarization— our new common language. The Internet has made us casually offensive (because the repercussions are mitigated) and quicker to speak. But dialogue is an activity of curiosity, cooperation, discovery, and learning rather than persuasion, competition, fear, and conflict. This is love, and it is increasingly rare.

Some useful statements to pocket to create safe spaces for discussion:

Tell me more about that.
Tell me how your thoughts progressed in this.
I appreciate your experience with this. I'm listening.

I hear what you are saying.

I would love to learn from you.

I care about how you feel and your perspective here.

I understand that. I identify with that.

What do you think of _____?

I hadn't thought of it in that way. Thank you for that angle.

Let me think about that a bit before I respond. Thanks for your transparency.

We listen sincerely; we don't just reload while someone else's mouth is moving. Dialogue is easily spooked, so you must be vigilant against fear, dismissal, manipulation, and apathy—true enemies of safe dialogue. You'll feel it at first, deep down, the urge to rebut, rebuke, refute. It will be a cold rock in your gut, tempting you to correct or disagree, or to be offended and center yourself in that person's story. But that instinct can be overcome, and the results of someone feeling heard and respected are immediate and palpable. It takes a fairly high level of humility, empathy, and courage to keep a space open and healthy. It is a developed skill that takes practice.

To me, that is what love looks and feels like. The Christian cliché "love the sinner, hate the sin" is problematic because it is always long on judgment and short on love. People sense that deeply; they understand when a relationship is fundamentally unsafe, precariously balanced on a scale of disapproval. Maybe not today, maybe not tomorrow, but eventually, a fork in the road will come, and the rejection will be painful beyond measure. I am in a couple of relationships exactly like that, except I am the one on the ropes. I hold back from investing because I know the inevitable end game. I am steeling myself against desertion. As kind and polite as these relationships are now, they feel very different from my friendships that are forever, regardless, despite anything, permanent. I don't know how to explain it, but my soul knows the difference.

It is not my responsibility to change other people, nor them me. It just isn't. It never was. Remember, the plan involves a heavy, obscene amount of love on my part, but I can take the task of "fixing someone" entirely off the table, permanently. I'm free to love him or her without stipulation, which creates a much wider, safer space to actually let God do what God does, which is redeem all of our lives into glory.

You have this permission, dear one. Can you hear it? *Snip, snip, snip.* The sound of the strings attached to love clipped right off. No strings. You can love truly, without conditions, without agenda, without a fork in the road, without disapproval, without fear, without obligation. You can love someone with a different ideology, different religious conviction, different sexual identity, ideas, background, ethnicity, opinions, different anything. You can love someone society condemns. You can love someone the church condemns. You have no other responsibility than to represent Jesus well, which should leave that person feeling absurdly loved, welcomed, cherished. There is no other end game. You are not anyone's savior; you are a sister.

Love is a genuine solution. It breaks down barriers and repairs relationships. It invites in the lonely and defeats shame. It provides the lighted path to forgiveness, which sets everyone free. Love makes us brave, pulls up seats to the table, defuses bigotry, and attacks injustice. It is our most powerful spiritual tool. Do not underestimate it as the solution to almost everything that is broken.

We have only a few days on earth in the scope of history. We get one shot at this, one chance to live in a way that brings true honor to God, the great Lover of people. After Jesus's sacrifice, we became the cornerstone of His plan to embody good news as living demonstrations of His character. It is a humbling task with eternal consequences, and may it be said of our generation that we loved well. Just like we were taught. Just like we received.

Makeup can only make you look *pretty* on the *outside*, but it doesn't help if you are *ugly* on the *inside*. Unless you eat that makeup.[1]

–AUDREY HEPBURN

MY SOUL MATE NETFLIX

Gather round, young ones, and I will tell you a tale that will frighten and confuse you. It will sound like something from the Dark Ages, ye days of old. You will wonder: *What sort of life was that? How did they survive?* Those of us who struggled through will tell you stories of triumph, of heroic juggling; you will gain a new respect for your ancestors born in the seventies.

See, once upon a time, there was no such thing as Netflix. No Hulu, no Primetime on Demand, no Apple TV, no Amazon Instant Video. These were fantastical inventions of a time well past the year 2000 (which, in our imaginations, included hover-crafts and time travel). We had what was called "basic cable," which meant that shows aired on four channels on a certain day at a certain time. And that is the end of the tale.

If you wanted to watch, for example, *Magnum P.I.* with your mom, then you had to be parked on the couch on Thursdays at 8:00 p.m. or miss Magnum and T.C.'s shenanigans while Higgins tried to maintain some bloody decorum. You got one shot at your show, and if you got home late because your mom's Jazzercise class went long, then you had to call your friend for a recap. Side note: Young Ones, telephones were attached to the wall with a cord back then, so you stretched it into the pantry for some privacy, away from your mom's nosy interference, while hollering, "This isn't Communist Russia, Mom—or, should I say, GORBACHEV!" (This is how children of the Cold War aired grievances.)

Back then, there weren't channels dedicated to subcategories of the population. There was no Disney channel, no Food Network, no ESPN, no Bravo. There was Sam Donaldson, Peter Jennings, and, my personal crush, Tom Brokaw on the news, and we got cartoons for three hours on Saturday mornings until CBS switched to golf at 11:00 after the Smurfs. Oh sure, MTV hit the scene in 1981, but we couldn't watch it because of the devil. Apparently we could watch a show starring two outlaw brothers, their half-naked cousin, and a car painted with the Confederate flag but couldn't watch Madonna sing "Like a Virgin" because we might get secondhand pregnant.

We got a taste of the future when VCRs finally became affordable for regular people. We could tape our shows! We set it on top of our enormous console TV encased in faux wood and perched on a fancy swivel. The only teeny downside was that our model didn't allow us to schedule the recording; someone still had to put the tape in and press record as the show aired. This involved panic, calling your neighbor, and begging her to break into your house to press record so you wouldn't miss *Moonlighting* while you were at church choir practice. And heaven help if she accidentally taped over *The Masters*, because Dad would relaunch a dissertation on proper labeling and respect for intellectual property.

I probably need counseling over the tape situation. For a while, VHS tapes only had two or three available hours, so you'd throw in a half-used tape to record *Kids Incorporated*, come back later that night to watch it, and it would cut off right in the middle of a crucial moment when Stacy (i.e., Fergie) considered smoking a cigarette given to her by an unsavory traveling rock band member because she was *sick and tired* of being treated like a child, like we all were, man. Did she smoke the cigarette? Did she become an addict? Did Gloria and The Kid talk her out of it? We never knew. (The online synopsis of *Kids Incorporated* says: "A group of kids sing songs at a club for kids. They solve problems in between performances." This was my dream job description in 1986.)

We thought we'd arrived when TiVo launched a few months' shy of the year 2000. We made it to The Future, and it was everything we hoped for minus the jet cars! Sure, Y2K was looming and we were hoarding milk jugs of water and canned corn, but besides the end of the world, it seemed the absolute height of entertainment technology, and we were having it. Schedule recordings with a remote control, fast-forward through commercials, and never miss another minute of *Who Wants to Be a Millionaire* . . . yes, please! An entire generation of young mothers started putting their children to bed again with patience and nurture, no longer throwing kids into beds with four-word prayers because *Friends* started at 8:00 and it was 7:57. It was an imperfect system for my friend Molly, who kept an actual spreadsheet of her shows on all networks (carefully curated through *TV Digest*) and had to delete three programs a day to make room for new scheduled recordings, but she was up for this sort of aggressive TV watching and approached it with the dedication of an Olympian.

What more could there be? How could anyone improve on this system? You and I both know, my friends. Let's say it together: Netflix. I don't want to overstate it, but Netflix is my soul mate. Like Steely Dan said: I have found my home at last. Any show, any network, movies, UK programming, original series, all in a digital library that is surely a foreshadowing of heaven. Easily the best feature in the Netflix Rolodex of awesomeness:

Binge watching.

Episode after episode, all in glorious succession with no commercials and only a ten-second window in which to end the binge and get your life back together, which you loosely consider during seconds one through seven, but then the next episode automatically begins and it's too late. What are we supposed to do? Turn it off at that point? We're not Communists. The fates decided for us, and so, with forbearance, we move on to episode eleven of *Gilmore Girls* and log our fifth straight hour on the couch. After you auto-start the fourth episode, even Netflix itself throws shade with a pop-up screen: *Do you want to continue watching?* YES, I DO, NETFLIX. I don't need your shame. Pretty judgy for an entertainment platform that offers 132 episodes of *Xena: Warrior Princess*. Don't act like you're concerned about our mental intake.

Admittedly, a quick survey of the scene communicates some slothfulness: potato chip crumbs on your shirt, an empty takeout container, a dirty cup (Diet Coke when you started at 9:00 p.m.), a red-stained glass (wine now that it is 1:23 a.m.), a cell phone you called your children on to tell them to go to bed, wadded up tissues from Rory's graduation speech in Stars Hollow. Fine, it isn't our best look. We can't always be awesome.

But the occasional guilt-free Netflix binge is delightful. Sydney and I watched four seasons of *Downton Abbey* in two days over Christmas break one year. We snuggled under a quilt and made tea for twelve hours a day. Brandon and I ripped through *Friday Night Lights*, *Parenthood*, *Mad Men*, and *Arrested Development*. He and the boys knocked off *Lost* in two weeks one summer (not sure they showered), and I was the lone soldier forging through *Unbreakable Kimmy Schmidt*, *Gilmore Girls*, *Broadchurch*, and *30 Rock*.

The upside: we don't watch any shows in real time, so our TV is off all day. Downside: when Brandon and I binge watch a new series, our house looks like an episode of *Hoarders*, and it's like we're raising creepy Children of the Corn with unwashed hair and haunted eyes of neglect: *Will there be anything for dinner tonight, Mother and Father? Or shall we eat the rats in the barn?*

Well, God bless. Everyone is entitled to a Netflix binge now and again. No one will die from it, and if our kids can't pour themselves cereal for dinner for three straight nights, they need to get some home training. Just in case you are the reasonable sort, I thought I'd include a recipe you can make for dinner, set on the kitchen counter, and let your people consume for a couple of days. This is great on day one and even better on day two . . . right around the time you move into season three and cannot be bothered with getting up for the bathroom, much less someone's hunger.

PANANG CHICKEN CURRY

I make this on nights I have only twenty minutes for prep, because I am a very busy person. *Breaking Bad* will not watch itself. This is as easy as "spaghetti night" and infinitely yummier. Every one of my kids loves it. Brandon is the lone holdout on curry, which is a discernment problem he needs to work out. This recipe makes enough for a big family like mine plus leftovers. Feel free to cut it down if you hate delicious food in your fridge.

> 2 to 3 tablespoons olive oil
> Whatever veggies you have, sliced thin (my faves in
>   this recipe: snap peas or green beans, red or green
>   bell peppers, onions, and mushrooms, but truly,
>   whatever)

Salt to taste

A few shakes of curry powder, if you have it

2 to 4 tablespoons Panang curry paste* (to taste: less = less spicy, more = *muy caliente*. I have a bunch of Ethiopians and Texans in my house, so we like to burn.)

1 to 2 teaspoons Kaffir lime powder*

1 tablespoon fish sauce*

3 (13- to 14-ounce) cans coconut milk

2 cups veggie or chicken stock

1 pound chicken breasts, sliced super-duper thin (or shrimp or beef or tofu or no meat)

1 tablespoon cornstarch for a thicker curry

3 tablespoons water

Rice cooked to package directions, including serving size for your family (not only do I make extra for leftovers, but I put another can of coconut milk in my rice liquid, because I like to live dangerously. I recently pulled out a rice cooker I've had for five years and never used. So basically my life is changed).

Fresh basil, if you have it

Heat the olive oil in a stock pot over medium-high heat. When the oil is shimmering, add the veggies, sprinkle them with salt, and stir for 2 to 3 minutes. I add a few shakes of curry powder, too, because my mantra on spice is "more is more." Add the curry paste and lime powder. Stir into the oil and veggies until incorporated and no longer pasty. Add the fish sauce, coconut milk, and stock. Whisk. Add the sliced raw chicken. (I like the chicken poached in the curry instead of cooked before. Tough chicken makes me want to become a vegetarian. Okay, no it doesn't. But if you are a Nervous

Nelly about this, cook your chicken while you stir fry your veggies at the beginning. It's a free country.)

Simmer the curry for around 15 minutes. I usually make a little slurry of cornstarch whisked into cold water and add it to thicken up the curry a bit.

Into a bowl: rice, curry, chopped basil.

Chef's Serving Notes:

Go heavy on the liquid part of the curry when you dish it out, because this is the stuff dreams are made of. I am so serious.

Make extra, because your family can eat this for days while you knock off the fifth season of *Parenthood*.

*You can order the Panang curry paste, Kaffir lime powder, and fish sauce on Amazon. They will come straight to your doorstep. You're welcome.

We are the music
makers, and we
are the *dreamers*
of dreams.[1]

–FROM ODE BY
ARTHUR O'SHAUGHNESSY,
QUOTED BY WILLY WONKA

CHAPTER 10

MAKERS AND DREAMERS

Here's the thing: after you have had children in elementary school since 2003, you struggle to stay the course by the fifth kid. (Side note: For those of you mamas who haven't yet proceeded past elementary with your kids, here is some truth. Getting triplets applied, scholarshipped, admitted, and graduated from Harvard, Yale, and Princeton is less work than K–5. Elementary school is the mother's gauntlet; if you can survive it, you can survive anything. Middle school and high school are approximately eleventy billion times easier. For you. I don't even know what classes my big kids are in. I barely know what grades they are in.)

Anyway, my point is, my last child is finishing elementary school, and I'm not as "attentive" as I once was. Consequently, I often find out what she is learning when I clean out her backpack once every three weeks. Maybe this is because I just skim the newsletters; maybe it's because I rarely look in The Folder. These things are hard to discern.

Upon a belated cleanout recently, I discovered an extensive Dream Poster complete with printed photos (where did she get those?), captions, and a detailed account of her projected adult life. Unable to narrow her career options to one (this is quintessential Remy), she predicted her professional titles would include: Pastor, Writer, Singer, Dancer, and Artist. When I asked her about her wide array of dreams, she said, "I just want to make beautiful things."

I couldn't help it. I grinned. I deeply, intrinsically understand this. I, too, just want to make beautiful things. Don't you? Don't we want our lives to be lovely and creative and productive and meaningful? Don't we want to offer exquisite, sacred things to the world? This draw toward creation is important, worthy of our time and attention and nurture. We have these magnificent minds and hands and ideas and visions, and they beg us to pay attention, give them permission, give them life.

I sincerely believe we are created by a Creator to be creative. This is part of His image we bear, this bringing forth of beauty, life, newness. This bears out in one thousand different ways: we write, sculpt, paint, speak, dance, craft, film, design, photograph, draw, bring order, beautify, garden, innovate, produce, cook, invent, fashion, sing, compose, imagine. It looks like art, it looks like music, it looks like community, it looks like splendor. That thing in you that wants to make something beautiful? It is holy.

So let's start there: you are worthy and capable of creating. Full stop. Making art or literature or music isn't reserved for the elite. We are all seeded with creative gifts and the corresponding urges to bring them forth. I know that craving so well; it feels like a balloon expanding in my chest, filled with words, filled with ideas, filled with longing. For me, there is no relief from the pressure except to write. The exchange between creativity and expression is incredibly fulfilling, even if not one other eye ever reads those words.

There is something courageous about acknowledging your ability and right to create, even in the midst of "a real job" or mothering or managing. Women have the innate capacity to nurture their own art without a paycheck, audience, outside permission, or charitable intentions. Do you understand what I mean by charity? You are not required to save the world, or anyone for that matter, with your art. It isn't valuable only if it rescues or raises money or makes an enormous impact. It can be simply for the love of it. That is not frivolous or selfish in the slightest. If the only person it saves is you, that's enough.

The expanding balloon in your chest requires a few things. Time, for instance. Creating takes minutes and hours. Living a creative life means making room to dream, craft, compose, produce. It often requires a firm rejection of martyrdom, and I mean that sincerely. The narrative we accept sometimes includes prioritizing all other humans, tasks, and line items to the exclusion of creativity. *How dare I?* we ask. *There are more pressing needs in my life than this artistic expression.*

I am here to tell you with certainty: if you wait until you have natural margin to create, you will go to the grave empty-handed. I wrote my first book with two kids in diapers and one in pull-ups. It was absurd, obscene, a fool's errand. The expanding balloon demanded my partnership, so I did what all creatives do when their art is not their profession: I figured it out. I treated it like a calling. I was not remotely set up to be a career writer, but that is not why you start creating. It can't be. I didn't even start with an inkling of that notion.

If you want to produce something, if the balloon is filling, go ahead and create your thing. There, permission granted. This first step is a doozy. If you are waiting for someone to beg you to do the work or promise to give you a huge paycheck or rearrange your schedule to clear the time or somehow make this whole part easier, you might as well take your little dream for a long drive into the country and say goodbye. Creators create. It is one of their main characteristics, as a point of fact. Makers don't wait for someone else to tell them they should or can. They already know they should and they can.

Next, sorry to deliver this news, but *creating requires work.* Kind of hard, brutal, sanity-threatening work sometimes. All the dreams and ideas in your head have to transition to your hands, and I'm afraid there is no other way. Art requires time, which, of course, you have none of. This is the creator's dilemma. You will not miraculously produce by carrying on exactly like you are. It's a whole thing, and you have to make room for it.

Maybe that time for you is in the earliest wee hours, which is when legions of creators make the magic happen. Maybe you engineer a child swap or childcare to generate time. Maybe you let something go and free up a slot. Know this: *something will have to give.* I mean that sincerely. Creating will take time away from other things: sometimes kids, sometimes a spouse, sometimes a thing you used to do, sometimes sleep. Work does this. You don't get to keep everything as is and also add creativity. I have to regularly tell my kids this truth:

ME: I'll be in my office working.
KIDS: What do you even do out there? (If you think ten
    books will up your credibility at home, think again,
    grasshopper.)
ME: I'm writing. It is my work, and it is a real job.
KIDS: *side eye*
ME: IT IS.

Of course my kids wish I would devote every second to keeping them in the center of the universe, but creators create and creating is work and work takes time. And listen: art and innovation is good work. It means something. It is noble and important. It always has been.

I cried a river when my mom went back to college when we were in elementary, middle, and high school because she was less available to manage our whims, but it soon became a source of great pride for me, because I watched my mom do meaningful, hard work that mattered. She went for it, right in the middle of living life. I needed a mom who mothered, dreamed, worked, and achieved. We all did. Her creative environment was the classroom, and thank goodness she heeded the expanding balloon, because she touched and changed thousands of kids' lives during the next twenty-five years.

Finally, one last key point to remember as we talk about creating is that everyone wants to be famous or important but fewer want to work on their craft. Take a class, take a course, go to a conference (this is both how I developed and initially got published), join an artist group, study creators you admire in your genre, invite constructive criticism, pay attention to what good art does: *How does it use language? How does it convey emotions? What are the obvious elements? What are the intangibles? How does it move the story along? How does it develop? How does it sound? How does it look? How does it feel?* Notice what inspires *you* and moves *you* and speaks to *you*.

Do you know where I encountered my first vision for becoming a writer? What's that? The Bible? Oh no, sweet reader: *A Girlfriend's Guide to Pregnancy*. I read it in 1998 while pregnant with my oldest, and for the very first time I realized it was possible to write on a serious nonfiction subject (childbirth in this case, Jesus in mine) in a funny-funny-funny, friend-next-door, sometimes tender, and often inappropriate way. I guffawed and boohooed my way through Vicki Iovine's book, and as I closed the last page, I remember thinking: *This is how I've always wanted to write*, a thought I'd never actually had until it entered my mind fully formed.

A savvy reader might notice the similarities, in fact, between my inspiration book and my actual first book written five years later: *A Modern Girl's Guide to Bible Study*. They say imitation is the sincerest form of flattery, but I hedged closer to outright plagiarism as the working title was *A Girlfriend's Guide to Bible Study*, which we were forging ahead with until I got a cease-and-desist letter from Vicki Iovine's lawyer, a moment that should have mortified me but instead caused me to squeal: I GOT A LETTER FROM VICKI!!

To this day, almost twenty years after I picked up that book, when readers tell me we could be "best friends," a plunging sense of gratitude spreads through my chest, because my inaugural inspiration came from another writer who made a living as a (trademarked!) girlfriend, guiding her readers through shared experiences with humor, candor, and warmth. I learned truth from Jesus, but I learned tone from Vicki. When you tell me I feel like a friend, I can't explain what a deep compliment you are paying me, because my first true north as an author was not as an expert or theologian or authoritarian teacher but as an honest friend in the trenches with my readers.

I still draw from several categories of mentorship, because the day I stop learning is the day I need to hang it up. I regularly read books on the craft of writing, some a dozen times each. I start every day reading news articles, theological essays, positions opposite mine, and current-event commentaries. I cannot be a leader in any capacity without paying attention. I constantly reach for introspective, quiet spiritual practitioners like Henri Nouwen and Richard Rohr because they help steady the wild, dramatic, wordy compass I was born with. I devour humor writing like it is my job, mostly far outside the Christian subcategory. I cannot even imagine where I would be if David Sedaris, Tina Fey, and Erma Bombeck had not instructed me in the ways of satire. I also shut down my laptop and get out in the world, because academia has its place but can atrophy a real life. I need to see and smell and travel and put my arms around human beings. I cannot write a good story if I am not living one.

Doctors put in the work to be good doctors. Teachers do the work to be phenomenal teachers. Budding creators cannot imagine themselves beyond the need for development or unworthy of the investment, paycheck or no paycheck. Worry less about getting recognized and more about becoming good at what you do. Take yourself seriously. Take your art seriously. You are both worth this.

And by the way, do not become immobilized by good art already out there. Stop that this instant. I did everything out of order on my first book; not until the manuscript was finished did I comb the shelves looking for "comparable titles" for my "book proposal" (these were things I'd never heard of a hot day in my life). I remember standing in the aisle of a bookstore, running my fingers along book after book in my genre, thinking, *Oh my heavenly stars. My book has already been written by famous and smart people.* I could barely bring myself to peek inside them, terrified at how much better they were than mine. I went home and told Brandon, "It's over. There's no room for me."

But . . . there was.

There is no scarcity in creativity. The world always needs good offerings. We cannot have too much beauty. There is no such thing as too much wisdom and literature and story and craftsmanship. There is room for you. Don't be intimidated by successful makers; be inspired by them. Creativity doesn't divide but multiply, finding new expressions in everyone inspired by someone else's gift. We can draw from our favorite writers, artists, musicians, thinkers, leaders, teachers; they sharpen and stretch us, laying pavement for our own gifts, offering possibility and permission to be even better versions of our own creative selves. No need to feel threatened or minimized by someone else's amazing talents. It is all fed by the same river that has no end, no threshold, no limits.

Draw from your treasured mentors and then create what only you can; there is no one else who can do exactly what you do in the way you do it. Your story is yours alone. No one has already claimed your seat at the table no matter how similar the genre. Do your time; there is room for you.

Final note: just because one person says your work is crap doesn't mean it is. Or maybe it is, but that is not the end of your story. You cannot bail with your first rejection, first critique, first outright troll, first rough patch. You'll be done by the end of the week. Applause is not your end game or, in any case, your motivation. It can't be. If approval replaced dedication as creativity's fuel, this world would be barren, empty, decidedly less lovely. Creating is a synonym for perseverance. Keep going, learn from criticism, ignore the haters, press onward. The Harry Potter series was rejected twelve times before it got picked up, and IT IS DOING OKAY NOW.

As a writer, I can promise you that getting published (or featured or awarded or recognized) will not make you miraculously happy, rich (oh my gosh), or validated. I'm laughing as I type that, because I know you are thinking, *Yes, it will. I don't care what you say.* It won't. I'm telling you. You'll still be in your weird mind wondering why your life is mostly the same. Traditional success doesn't fix you like you thought it would.

Listen to me: this is my twelfth published book, a couple made Important Lists, and I swear I still feel wonky and wobbly and nervous and like a poser. Every time I sit down to write, I wonder if I can pull it off this time. Then, miraculously, as I push the watching eyes and lists and expectations out of my mind and open my heart as wide as it will go and put my fingers on the keyboard, there it is: the craft, the joy, the magic.

As it turns out, the applause isn't as fulfilling as the work.

Art is worth every second. So here I am, creators, cheering you on. We need you. We need your stories and craftsmanship and gifts and courage. We need you to prioritize your creativity. We need brave, committed artists to decorate this hurting world with loveliness, to partner with God in making beautiful things. Erase these words—*selfish, frivolous, unimportant*—and replace them with these—*necessary, exquisite, courageous*.

Bring it forth.

The world awaits, dear ones.

We're all a little *weird*
and life's a little weird,
and when we find
someone whose weirdness
is *compatible* with ours,
we join up with them and
fall in mutual weirdness
and call it *love*.[1]

–DR. SEUSS

CHAPTER 11

DEFER AND PREFER

Dinner conversation last night:

BEN: Mom and Dad, do you guys French kiss?
REMY: Gross! That's what dogs do!
BRANDON: Only French dogs.
ME: Brandon, gosh.
SYDNEY: Then don't read Mom's books, you guys. She
      talks about sex.
CALEB: Oh, I know. "Have lots of sex." I read that *right
      next to the kid chapter!* Sick!
BEN: I wish I didn't know this!
REMY: What does that mean?
ME: JUST EAT YOUR FRIED RICE, YOU GUYS.
BRANDON: Hurry up and go upstairs so me and
      Mom can French.
SYDNEY: This is why we can't bring our friends over.

Sometimes I miss the days when our conversations revolved around Minecraft. When one births a shiny new baby, one does not envision that child discussing your sex life over Chinese food someday. (A friend recently told her five kids they were having another baby, and her sixteen-year-old daughter sobbed, "Do you guys not know what responsible intercourse is?!" Their fifteen-year-old daughter then burst into tears and wailed, "We're going to have to drive a church van!")

Parent Sex: delighting teenagers worldwide. Like I always tell our kids, after this many years, just be glad your parents still have sex and like each other. And this comforts them zero percent.

You guys, brace yourselves: Brandon and I got married at twenty-one and nineteen. (College sophomore reader? *I was your age.* Let it sink.) I was a literal teenager who couldn't even drink at her own wedding, not that we had any booze in the Baptist Fellowship Hall, but still. We have been married twenty-three years now; more than half my life. What we two fools were thinking marrying that young, I have no clue, because when I look at a nineteen-year-old girl now, I want to pet her hair and maybe rock her. Babies!

Allow me a few thoughts on marriage discovered the normal way: in hindsight.

First, the upside of being a child bride. We were both so young, so freshly launched in our own skin that we weren't yet entrenched in our habits, our passions, our preferences. The main scaffolding was in place: our devotion to Jesus and crazy, mad love. With the structural elements and a few load-bearing walls in place, something happened after the wedding:

We grew up together.

Rather than navigating our twenties as two individuals blending very developed lives together, we matured as one unit, writing a new adult story with our lives. I cannot imagine where I would be today at forty-two without Brandon helping me learn who I was at twenty-three. There is no part of my adult story that doesn't include his wisdom and balance, his perspective and discernment. There is no me without him. This is *our life*, every piece of it, each memory, every adult moment we built together.

As a bright reader, you've probably guessed there was also an underbelly to marrying so young. For instance, we banked just north of eleven thousand dollars our first year of marriage. That was our combined salary from two part-time jobs, and we suffered one of the biggest fights that year because Brandon bought chicken fingers from the Arby's drive-thru. WE AREN'T MILLIONAIRES, BRANDON. While that seems hilarious now, financial struggles are nothing to sniff at. We slogged and sloughed our way through poverty and emerged with some bad habits, some debt, some scars. We did not surface unscathed; I still operate out of a scarcity mentality that wore a groove into my financial psyche.

More important, that early on, we simply hadn't developed the building blocks of a happy union yet: compromise, communication finesse, selflessness, wisdom. These took time, and although we are still slowly acquiring them, we left many ugly words and regrettable decisions in our early wake. Could we have avoided them if we were older? Probably. I don't know. Those first couple of years are hard. They just are. Maybe all the first few years are wobbly. Two selfish people joining together for life is a miracle every time.

Almost two dozen years later, the communication part is still the biggest slice of the pie, the key element that tends to make or break us. It deeply affects our general sense of security and how much sex we are or are not having. And even after all these years, it is still work. We are not yet at that stage when marriage skips along seamlessly, a lifetime of spoken words smoothing the road and receding in importance, when a pat on the hand or a glance conveys everything necessary, muscle memory from decades of communication.

Nope. We're still climbing the mountain, trying to mix two different processing styles into one cohesive, happy marriage. It has helped immensely to prioritize self-awareness on personality traits and preferences, because although like-minded in tons of crucial ways, Brandon and I are basically processing opposites. In our early years, every conflict ended in an impasse, as we prefer two different routes toward the same conclusion:

BRANDON: What we need here is words. Lots of words. Millions of words immediately. We will speak whatever words are in our heads, however half-baked, and eventually they will lead us to the end.

ME: What we need here is to retire to our private quarters; think many, many thoughts about this internally; inwardly adjust behavior; and recover from the confrontation, then carry on with our lives.

What could go wrong?

Brandon is a verbal processor. He finds his ideas by talking them out. Rather than work stuff out in his head, he says the first sentence out loud, then continues until he reaches a resolution. Practically, this means he may say something early or midway through that doesn't match the ending. It isn't disingenuous; it is simply a half-formed thought that leads to a more-formed thought that leads to the conclusion. Consequently, for him talking is the only way through conflict; silence or space isn't time to sort things out—it is simply an unresolved black hole. The speaking part is essential to his process. That is the way his mind and ideas work. It is why he used to tape his skeletal notes on the glass door and talk out his sermons in the shower on Sunday mornings. Brandon's ideas find full formation verbally.

Likewise, his urgency and expediency is wrapped in intensity. According to him, it is proactive; according to me, aggressive. His tone is intense, posture intense, language intense, emotions intense, volume of words intense. This is not right or wrong; it is simply the way Brandon is wired. He is not a laid-back guy, which also means he gets stuff done, he works hard, he handles conflict, he is a great visionary. He is in Go Mode most of the time; his fuse is shortish but his reach is long.

I am an internal processor. I think three million thoughts until I say one of them out loud. I spend the majority of my life in my head. By the time I give voice to feelings or ideas, I have considered that thing from every angle one hundred times. This is slow and takes time, which, as it turns out, can be "frustrating" for a verbal processor who is completely on hold until I join back in. I think my way to conclusions, so by the time I get there, they are pretty cemented. Thus when I hear an idea halfway through that doesn't match the ending, it feels like a lie (*but you said . . . ?*). In contrast, my sermon notes are practically scripted, endless pages of ordered points, because my ideas find full formation internally through writing. I don't even leave 2 percent of a talk up to "verbal winging," because that is never how I make any sense. (Even typing that sent panic up my spine.)

Consequently, intense communication fries a circuit for me. It is all too immediate, too unconsidered, too many careless words flying around. I am like one of those fainting goats; I just freeze and keel over. Because I deal with life in my head, I am not comfortable navigating assertiveness, word overload, and half-formed ideas alongside conflict resolution. I feel manhandled, confused, or unheard. On the other side, Brandon feels ignored, disrespected, or punished.

Just understanding our opposite processes has been life changing. Without any self-awareness, all that's left is frustration, but acknowledging our basic operating systems removes the ancillary malice once assumed in conflict: bullying and insensitivity or withholding and disregard. Neither of us wants to harm. Ever. We aren't being difficult or obstinate. We don't want to punish each other. There is nothing wrong with either of us. This isn't some weird game with a winner and loser. We have no axe to grind in conflict.

We just work through ideas and feelings differently.

Worth noting, we virtually always come to the same conclusion, eventually. We are incredibly compatible across almost every subject and value. We both want intimacy and mutual respect and emotional safety in our marriage. We like the same things. We have the same kind of fun. We love the same friends. We pick out the same couch simultaneously. At the end of the day, we love each other equally and want the other to be happy and secure in this marriage.

So we work. Brandon, God love him, will sit quietly next to me and talk to me like a spooked cat: *May I have fifteen minutes to talk calmly about this thing?* He even loosens his physical posture as if to say: Look how easy breezy I am about this, everyone just be cool. Or he will give me notice, building in the time I seem to require: *Can we talk about this thing after the kids go to bed?* Excellent. This makes my brain so happy, and it will spend the next six hours getting ready.

In the midst of it all, my brain tries to tell my adrenaline: *No one ever died from a heated discussion. Get a grip, Hatmaker.* I force myself to stay in, to stay engaged, even to say words out of my mouth (!). I remember that what I interpret as aggression is simply a man who loves me, trying to fix something that is off. That's all it is. He just has a lot of feels and words about it, and I can handle that because I am a grown-up. I can meet him somewhere in the middle. It communicates love to him when I engage, telling him I care enough to see this thing through.

We have learned to accept each other's limits, especially when we raise the red flag signaling an impending meltdown. We can respect each other's thresholds and adjust accordingly now. After twenty-three years, we've discovered deference and preference—*deferring* to the other's process and *preferring* each other's needs. This comes naturally around 38 percent of the time, so that seems like a miracle. It's like Mother Teresa level; although, come to think of it, Mama T was never married; she was probably like, *A husband? Girl, please. I have WORK TO DO. Leave your feeling words at the door and hold this baby and kindly get out of my face.*

As it turns out, 38 percent (with a 62 percent *Mama tried* rate) means we are still pretty into each other. We French kiss and stuff. Brandon is still my favorite person, and we've built a beautiful shared life. Sisters, listen, we are still scaling the mountain with work and compromise, but at this point in the hike, I'm here to tell you the view is worth the climb. The fragile tipping points that once set us off are mostly smoothed out because, Lord have grace, we cannot feel strongly about everything. We've achieved a midlevel chill rate and are no longer jittery, high-maintenance young adults circling the drain about nonsense. Our base camp is more like: *I like you, I like this, I like us, sometimes not, but mostly yes.*

Around this stage of marriage, we've noticed a temptation to believe that another person, someone other than your spouse, would make life so much easier, so much better, so much less annoying and difficult, but that whole suggestion is based on faulty logic. There is a fake idea swirling around out there that says if marriage is hard, we're doing it wrong. If our person gets on our nerves or still does that one frustrating thing after two decades, moving on to a different man would fix everything that is difficult.

It's nonsense. Really. Rather than fantasizing about greener grass on some other side, *water your own grass first*, because there is no marriage, no union that doesn't have its share of aggravations and struggles. None, I promise. There is no man or woman immune to selfishness, mediocrity, laziness, or failure. Sure, Other Guy can seem quite shiny in that other yard (as could you at first), but a permanent relocation discloses the truth: grass is pretty much grass. Add in bills, parenting, and the lame responsibilities of real adulthood, and that shine wears off lightning fast. That grass is fake, untrampled by the wear and tear of an actual shared life. It is a lovely illusion that looks beautiful from afar but becomes sharp and artificial to the touch, if not initially, eventually. The ensuing wreckage will outpace the fantasy.

Between two people willing to work—and mutuality desperately matters; one soldier cannot win a marriage back alone—to fight for connectedness, to be honest and humble and say hard things and hear hard things, most marriages can be restored from even the worst breach. If you are lonely in your own marriage today, you are not alone, first off. Scratch under the surface of most unions, and you'll find a familiar song of struggle, one most of us have sung or are singing. It is no simple thing to commit to one person for your whole life and make it work. *Mother Teresa was on to something.* But I've seen God restore marriages that even I, the eternal optimist, declared doomed, beyond repair, in the grave. All I'm saying is that healing is possible between two truth-telling, committed people willing to hope for resurrection.

But please hear this: I never prioritize marriage over the healthy souls of the two individuals inside it; abuse, neglect, betrayal, violence—there are good and right reasons to leave sometimes. Not for one second do I think God would sacrifice your health, safety, or dignity on the altar of marriage. He did not create this beautiful mystery to protect an abuse of power. Sometimes one or both partners is so broken, the only healthy option is to dissolve and find individual healing. Marriage is not designed to make you forfeit your soul.

But when two people with bad habits, irritating routines, and personal baggage decide to look each another in the eye, own their own junk, defer and prefer the other, and work like it is their paying job, they can still gross their kids out by French kissing after twenty-three years and manage not just to love but to like each other too. It is absolutely a miracle, worth every millisecond of work, and one of life's most surprising and greatest gifts.

How To
(Part Two)

HOW TO PREPARE THE PERFECT MEAL EVERYONE IN THE HOUSE WILL LOVE

1. Go through all the recipes you've pinned on Pinterest but have never made. There are approximately 3,847 of them. Take your time.
2. Make a list of meals that are "winners." You never knew your Crock-Pot could be such a champion.
3. Prepare the grocery list of all the ingredients you don't have at home. This comprises around 92 percent of the required ingredients. You have never, in fact, bought bean sprouts, pomegranates, shrimp paste, or pickled beets. You aren't even sure what a kumquat is, but the picture on Pinterest looked pretty.
4. Go to the store.
5. Realize you forgot the list. WHY? Why is the list so hard to transport?

6. Buy another box of Lucky Charms, because that is what is for dinner. All week.

Programming Note: This gaffe might actually save you from the inevitable headache called Making New Food for My Family to Hate. Because you know what makes children happy? Lucky Charms for dinner.

HOW TO GET IN SHAPE

1. Buy an exorbitantly expensive outfit. Spend more on this than on the last six items of clothes combined, because a sports bra capable of containing your Golden Globes costs around $729 apparently.
2. Sign up for a ClassPass and head straight to that barre session your friends won't stop talking about. They can't all be wrong.
3. Lie there in confusion for forty-five minutes trying to find "the tuck" (which feels strangely similar to the way you hunch over your computer). What even is this? Someone made this class up. Who ever heard of *barre*? Is everyone too fancy for blue-collar sit-ups these days?
4. Feel like a baby giraffe when the instructor tells you to "tuck and plank" at the same time. (This instructor is a bad person. There is no way she is saved.)
5. Try not to look at yourself in the mirror because it is not your friend at this juncture. It is not kind. It is not giving you good news today.
6. Debate sneaking out no fewer than forty-seven times.
7. March your well-contained Hindenburgs next door for the

new 450-calorie nonfat Starbucks concoction. Your friends are whack.

HOW TO ENSURE PEOPLE FEEL COMPELLED TO POP IN FOR A VISIT

1. Don't do the dishes for a day and a half.
2. Toss your children's toys in every walking path of the house.
3. Put a piece of toast with peanut butter under the couch throw pillow so as not to be noticed until a guest is comfortably sitting down.
4. Place someone's underwear in an obscure but visible area.
5. Succumb to your child's demands for hard-boiled eggs, so your house smells like a diaper pail.
6. Dump four loads of laundry on your couch; this is obviously intended to be a folding zone for the clothes, but they will likely just become couch companions for the day, like another member of the family.
7. Have one or more children running around either covered in Sharpie, in tattered panties, or stark naked.
8. And, by all means, do not shower that day.
9. Happy hosting!

Programming Note: The above steps should ensure imminent drop-by company, but if these measures fail to summon the new friend you are trying to impress or your mother-in-law, start screaming like a lunatic at everyone or enjoy a complete Mom Meltdown, and your surprise guests will certainly be standing on your doorstep listening in on your crazy.

HOW TO GET UNINVITED BACK
TO A HOME DECOR STORE

1. Run in with your toddler for a "quick errand." Be sure to estimate this task as taking five minutes or less, which will ensure you don't bring in the diaper bag or any other tools of the trade.
2. Get distracted looking for a price tag on an item that caught your eye. (These stores trick you into betraying your five-minute timetable, and you would do well to commit that to memory. There is never a five-minute trip through Bed Bath & Beyond. Never. This is a unicorn. This doesn't exist. This has happened never. I'm trying to help you.)
3. Hear gasp from a bystander, and look up to see your son's bare behind and a hearty stream of urine trailing from the cart into a $48 decorative basket. You don't understand why he had to drop his underpants to his ankles, but in addition to soiling the home goods, he has now displayed his bits and bobbles for all to witness.
4. Panic as you realize step 1.
5. Watch the tee-tee run down the shelving unit and soak the towels below before pooling in a delightful puddle at the end of Aisle 7.
6. Calculate your expenditures to around ninety-five dollars of urine-soaked home items that now belong to you.
7. Congratulations. You can show back up to this store in five years.

HOW TO FIND A FAMILY PET

1. In an attempt to ward off the campaign, have your children read *Where the Red Fern Grows*, *Old Yeller*, and *Sounder*. As a

diversionary tactic, you want them to prematurely mourn the dog you do not want to purchase.

2. Understand that all promises to feed, walk, care for, and pooper scoop for said dog are false. These children are liars. They will fulfill their promises for approximately two months, at which point all bets are off. The dog is yours. It is your next child. Make your peace.

3. Visit the local shelter's Open House. Overestimate your willpower.

4. Look into the dark, loving eyes of the calmest dog there and fall hard. Throw in the towel. You're done. The campaigners have won.

5. Spend hours constructing an outdoor kennel for your new adoptee. After all, you are a woman with boundaries, and the dog *will* be living outside. This is obvious. You've made yourself clear here. A dog? Fine. But not an indoor dog. This is just how it is. Dogs are meant to live outside. This is a part of their breeding. They are outdoor animals like wolves and turtles. This is God's will.

6. Bring your pup home on a below-freezing day. Without emotion, allow him to "spend just his first night inside," because you have boundaries but you are humane, for the love. Just this once while he gets used to you.

7. On night two, realize this dog is never spending a night outside in his life. He owns everyone, you included. The dog is the victor. Go ahead and buy expensive pet food online full of probiotics for his digestive health. Change your Facebook profile pic. Rearrange your day so he won't be alone. Get a loyalty card at PetSmart. Make him a pallet at the end of your bed. You're a goner.

How to Have the Sex Talk with Your Elementary-Age Kid

1. When asked where babies come from, first say God.

2. When pressed, say Jesus.

3. When she wants to know how this actually works, have a small, internal panic attack. No one told you about this awkward moment when you were all, *I can't wait to be a moooooom!* Your mom just put a diagram on your nightstand with a box of tampons when you were twelve years old. You have no home training here.

4. Politely excuse yourself, grab the books you ordered two years ago for this moment, and send your husband in to do the heavy lifting because submission.

5. Listen at the door to lots of hilarious explanations and many, many uses of the words *penis* and *vagina*. Stifle laughter as your child calls it a *bergina*. Scold yourself for calling it a "bird" all these years like a weirdo. You've ruined her chance at ornithology.

6. Mask intense concern when husband comes out asking for a dry erase board and two dolls. This tutorial is obviously terrifying, but the only alternative is you talking about "special hugs," which was the next card you planned to play.

7. Fall flat on the ground when your daughter asks if sex "feels like a hot dog," and your husband replies, *"It's more like a summer sausage."* She can't unhear that. She is going to therapy. Start saving.

8. With all your might, maintain a straight face when she comes out forty-five minutes later, solemnly pats your arm, and says, "I kind of wish I didn't know that. Thanks for going through that mess to create me, Mom."

HOW TO MOTHER ADULT CHILDREN

1. Allow them to live past their teenage years. Congratulations on completing step 1!

2. Smile and choke back the "I told you so!" when they finally understand something you've been saying for *years*. This is really hard. Practice not rolling your eyes in the mirror. Show restraint like Jesus.

3. Resist the urge to yell, "What an idiot!" or its Christian cousin, "You reap what you sow" when they encounter hardships after ignoring your wise counsel, which they sought and pretended to listen to over homemade pie.

4. Laugh when they reminisce about your Mom Fails without citing their crazy-inducing shenanigans, as if you just spontaneously lost your crap. No, Adult Child, you sneaking vodka under the babysitter's nose or driving your truck into a light post while dishing up an elaborate lie regarding a pothole did not at all contribute to the Mom Fails.

5. If they have children, forget that you ever raised any kids and keep your reasonable but hopelessly old-fashioned suggestions to yourself, as they likely contradict the plethora of "experts" now available on Snapchat.

6. When said adult children have teenagers, comfort them as they navigate step 1, and graciously receive any tearful apologies for their childhood and young adult behavior (see steps 2 and 3). This is also the stage where it's safe to explain step 4, because at this point, they are finally all the way on your side. They've crossed over. They know the truth like only raising your own teenagers can deliver. They are here in the Land of the Knowing. Open wine and offer a toast for surviving each other. Call your own mother, and apologize again.

7. Always have the ingredients to make pie in case they stop in for a visit to request advice they may or may not take.

HOW TO GET THE PERFECT PROFESSIONAL PICTURE OF YOUR PRECIOUS ANGEL BABIES

1. Spend an exorbitant amount of time picking outfits that are just right. This should take entirely too much time, money, and energy. They need to coordinate but not match. Comb Pinterest for ideas to steal. (Southern mamas, check local rules about the age cutoff for boys in smocking or knickers. Pictures are forever. Please refrain from dressing your sixth-grade son in knee socks.)

2. Make sure they are groomed but not "I just this day got a haircut" groomed.

3. Scout out the perfect location, and time it just right for blooming tulips and late afternoon light. This should gobble up at least four afternoons.

4. Adjust naps slightly and time your forty-five-minute drive to the location so they can nap a bit on the way.

5. Load kids into the family truck *not* wearing their picture clothes. Don't forget the picture clothes, and don't forget to put the picture clothes as far away from kids as possible.

6. Play classical music on the way, meditate on a psalm, pray, promise Jesus all sorts of obedience if He will procure some goodwill. Remind Him that you are a good person and you don't ask for much. You just need this photo shoot to work, because it is costing five hundred dollars and the only pictures you have of their childhood are on your iPhone.

7. Get to the spot, change kids in the way back, grab your sippy cups and nonstaining snack bribes, and set the angels

down in just the right place. Try not to micromanage the
photographer but fail fairly epically.

8. Keep your tone light and airy as the kids start fighting and
whining: "No worries, everyone! Ha ha ha ha! Everything is
great! You're doing so great! You look great! Look at Mommy!
This is so fun! We're having so much fun here!"

9. Realize all three children looking at the camera at once
making a normal face is a fantasy. This photo shoot is
doomed. You try everything. You dance like a monkey. You
promise the moon and the stars. Soon, your bribes turn to
threats: "Smile right, or I'll give you something to cry about!"
You have sweat pouring down your back into your underwear.
Your anxiety has permeated the atmosphere, and even the
photographer despairs.

10. Get the proofs back two weeks later. They are mostly a
disaster. Your children look like robots. Or like human
children who never learned to smile naturally and only know
how to grimace, scowl, look off camera, fake smile. They look
like well-dressed, miniature serial killers.

11. Use candid iPhone shot of your family at a football game for
your Christmas card.

Sometimes, I feel *discriminated* against, but it does not make me *angry*. It merely astonishes me. How can any deny themselves the *pleasure* of my company? It's beyond me.[1]

–ZORA NEALE HURSTON

CHAPTER 12

SANCTUARY

I have a colorful father-in-law. He grew up in Oak Ridge, Tennessee, as a quintessential 1950s teen, a track runner and football player at UT in Knoxville, then straight into the army where he retired as a first sergeant twenty-four years later. I regularly keep my notepad handy when we're together, because, out of the clear blue yon, Bob Hatmaker will jumpstart conversations like this:

"When I was a teenager, Bobby Tichner and I used to go squirrel hunting before school. We were always late to school, but at least we got fried squirrel that night!"

"It was 1965. I was in Germany, and I found a couple of I-talian girls . . ."

"In 1957, I visited my friend Mikey Ryder at Tulane during Mardi Gras. Everyone had bottles up their sleeves. I remember about thirty minutes of it."

These stories are endless and delightful, a daughter-in-law's thrill and a writer's dream. Most of Bob's tales are wildly entertaining, but there is some real tenderness too. He told of his small church in rural Tennessee where he and his buddies were surrounded by deacons, pressed on all sides, and terrified into receiving salvation during a church service. Strong-willed and resistant to spiritual bullying, Bob alone refused to "walk the aisle." The pastor threw his hands up and proclaimed, "Well, I've done all I can do with this one. I guess he's going to hell." Bob walked out that door and never looked back.

It was the last time he went to church regularly—more than sixty years ago.

Who could blame him?

Sometimes the one place we should all be most welcomed is the very place we are most rejected; the house of healing becomes the inflicter of pain. Much like any betrayal, the more considerable the source, the harder the loss. No one can wound us more than those supposed to nurture: our parents, our spouses, our churches. The chasm between expectation and reality is particularly grim in supposed safe places.

As I've written often, my history with the church is complicated. It spans my entire life and, like any long-term relationship, has had its ups and downs. As a pastor's daughter and wife, I've seen too much behind the curtain to idolize the church. It is a form meant to bring order to and strengthen the Good News; it is not the Good News itself. It is only the wineskin, not the wine; one of the containers, not the substance.

It's an important distinction, because for many, it is tempting to worship the church, removing the inherent safety of the sanctuary and prioritizing the structures instead, at which point the people become a commodity instead of the body. By definition, a sanctuary is "any holy place of refuge" and, more specifically, "a sacred place where fugitives were entitled to immunity from arrest." In other words, the guilty, the outcast, the refugee, the criminal, the desperate—all safe from harm or punishment under the steeple, protected within its four walls.

Of course, the inner sanctuary, deep in the belly of the temple, was once only available to the religious elite, the priests, the high and holy Levitical bloodline. No sin could cross the threshold into God's presence there, and the purification process in which a priest was permitted entry once a year was complicated and wrought. But listen:

> We have this hope as an anchor for the soul, firm and secure. It enters the inner sanctuary behind the curtain, where our forerunner, Jesus, has entered on our behalf. . . . Therefore, brothers and sisters, since we have confidence to enter the Most Holy Place by the blood of Jesus, by *a new and living way opened for us* through the curtain, that is, his body, and since we have a great priest over the house of God, let us draw near to God with a sincere heart and with the full assurance that faith brings, having our hearts sprinkled to cleanse us from a guilty conscience and having our bodies washed with pure water. Let us hold unswervingly to the hope we profess, for he who promised is faithful. (Hebrews 6:19–20; 10:19–23, emphasis added)

We're in, man.

Jesus permanently made the sanctuary safe, pure, and accessible to all. He didn't lessen its holiness but rather raised us to heaven's standards through the cross. It's just crazy. It was truly a new and living way, and Jesus threw the church doors open to the entire world and bid us *come*. Obviously, this entire miracle was Jesus's doing: His life, His death, His resurrection, His dreams for this earth.

There is no such thing as a human hierarchy to approach God anymore. That old system is gone; Jesus completely leveled the field of humanity. There are no gatekeepers, there is no "us" and "them," no tricky steps or tricky people to get through. No human being can decide who is in and who is out. We're all the same now, brothers and sisters in one family, and Jesus is the entire substance of the church—our front door, our baptism, our High Priest, our bread and wine.

Nor is there a prototype for admission or, in any case, for sanctioned blessing. In many American churches, the approved stereotype for fully included members is Married (just once!) with Children. Most ministries and sermons and language and structures revolve around the 1950s family model. Obviously, there is a place for this work, as large segments of the population are indeed married with children. But *sanctuary* means all are safe, equally valued, everyone ministered to and included.

On a macro level, this includes singles both young and old, the divorced, married without kids, single with kids, empty nesters, LGBTQ singles, LGBTQ marrieds, widows and widowers, students. Parents of children with special needs, people with complicated families, couples with failing marriages, parents with wayward kids. People in a minority culture or minority race. Folks in these demographics regularly discuss how difficult it is to fit into the typical church, often feeling sidelined or tokened or dismissed. The Marrieds with Children are generally centered, and everyone else is a one-off.

On a micro level, and let's speak specifically about women, there are additional deviations from the norm that complicate embrace in the church: those who are assertive, academic, breadwinners, spicy, heady not girly, opinionated, gifted in leadership, those with a seedy past, those with a seedy present. Women with powerful careers, powerful ministries, powerful personalities.

Outside the sanctioned category, sometimes the church doesn't know what to do with the other women.

One of my first speaking engagements to a crowd larger than thirty was at an enormous, traditional church for the Sunday morning sermon. *The Sunday morning sermon in front of three thousand people, you guys.* As I was on the brink of hyperventilation on the front row, the pastor's assistant leaned over, two minutes before the service started, and whispered: "Did you know we've only had a woman give the Sunday morning message once in our entire history? And the funny thing is, a bunch of people stood up and walked out!"

YES. THAT IS FUNNY. YOU AND I THINK THE SAME THINGS ARE FUNNY, LADY. I try not to be petty, but I asked God to punish her for the timing of that comment, and I'd like to believe He did. (Anne Lamott says that "you know you've made God in your image when He hates all the same people you do."[1]) Church can be so weird for women. A woman with a PhD can operate on a person's brain stem but remain shut out of leading a church group because of her lady parts.

The thing is, we all want to belong, we all crave sanctuary, we are all invited guests. Women, I commission us to fix this. Rather than waiting for the church to get secure with everyone (Jesus's Church: Uncomfortable and Socially Awkward Since AD 33), *we* can set a bigger table for our sisters. We can pull up chairs, set out more plates, open extra wine. It is sacred work to open our eyes wide and look around: Who is unseen? Who is left out? Who is marginalized? Whose voice is silenced? Whose story is outside the lines? Who would feel isolated by the primary language here?

For those of us in the dominant narrative, it means not defaulting to our own demographic. Just like a white person is so embedded in majority culture, he or she has to deliberately seek racism to see it, the Marrieds with Children must choose to pay attention to folks outside the mainlined category. It is natural to filter language, community, needs, and perspectives through our own grid, but a simple mental channel change would expose how many of our church structures are isolating and narrow.

When I'm sitting by my gay friends in church, I hear everything through their ears. When I'm with my recently divorced friend, I hear it through hers. This is good practice. It helps uncenter us (which is, you know, the whole counsel of the New Testament) and sharpens our eye for our sisters and brothers. It trains us to think critically about community, language, felt needs, and inclusion, shaking off autopilot and setting a wider table. We must examine who is invited, who is asked to teach, who is asked to contribute, who is called into leadership. It is one thing to "feel nice feelings" toward the minority voice; it is something else entirely to challenge existing power structures to include the whole variety of God's people.

This is not hard or fancy work. It looks like diversifying small groups and leadership, not defaulting to homogeny as the standard operating procedure. Closer in, it looks like coffee dates, dinner invites, the warm hand of friendship extended to women or families outside your demographic. It means considering the stories around the table before launching into an assumed shared narrative. It includes the old biblical wisdom on being slow to speak and quick to listen, because as much as we love to talk, share, and talk-share some more, there is a special holiness reserved for the practice of listening and deferring.

My sister has been married to the guy of our dreams, Zac, for ten years. This is the man who named his slightly trashy backyard "Zacapulco" (complete with signage) and inspired our entire family to dub our patios with this inventive brand of tropical irony, resulting in "Hat-O-Vallarta," "Kingcun," and "Cabo san Drewcus" (our friends Andy and Anna Melvin loved our game and named their outdoor porch "Cozumelvin"). Anyhow, like millions of couples, Cortney and Zac have struggled to conceive, and I am regularly shocked at how many invade this tender space with gross insensitivity: *When are y'all finally going to have a baby? I guess you just don't want any kids to mess up your fun life, huh? Chop chop, you guys! Time to get going on those babies!* The whole notion of heartache, loss, or even basic privacy doesn't even register to people who assume others fit their template, and if they don't yet, they just need some prodding.

When our spiritual spaces are homogenous, it silences the hundreds of alternative stories that experience vibrancy or suffering outside the "norm." (As a full-time career gal, I sometimes feel the tremors of disapproval, because I've defected from the party line.) My dream is for a safe church, a wide table, no secondary kid tables. If Jesus made the sanctuary free and available for all, we should too. If the Savior of the World decided that demarcations and hierarchies and power players were no longer necessary to the health of his church, then who are we to reinstate a ranking system after Jesus rendered it obsolete?

Girls, if you reside outside the approved label of Docile Wife-Mom, first of all, I've never mastered "docile" a day in my life so, you know, solidarity. But I want you to hear me say that you are welcome here: in my space, in God's beautiful church, in this family of brothers and sisters. Your voice matters, your presence is imperative, and your story makes broad the body of Christ, which only strengthens the tribe, never weakens. (And Docile Wife-Moms? You are fully welcome too! We all count. Everyone counts. Everyone is in.)

Also, if your husband or family or kid or marriage or history or best friend or parent or personality or passion or orientation or career places you "outside the camp," I want to whisper something awesome to you: *there is no camp.* There is only Jesus and His band of scalawags and ragamuffins. Find your people. They exist. Raise your voice, tell your story, take your place. So many sojourners with your story or temperament need you to stand tall and strong; you represent many others, trust me. It only seems like everyone is all the same. But peek over your fence, look out into the big, beautiful world, and you will find it is wide and diverse and fascinating, and every sort of person thrives in God's kingdom.

Sure, maybe the Bob Hatmakers of the world cause some pearl clutching under the steeples, what with the I-talian girls and squirrel hunting and rough edges and proclivity to fish on Sunday mornings instead of don a tie, but I can assure you the church would have been better for his presence, his inclusion, because he is a good man and a loyal husband and father and a faithful neighbor and he had lovely gifts to offer had he been welcomed instead of banned all those years ago. It was our loss.

Let's set that wrong right by welcoming in the whole array of God's beloved.

What a beauty that church will be.

I don't exercise. If *God* had wanted me to bend over, he would have put *diamonds* on the floor.[1]

–JOAN RIVERS

CHAPTER 13

ON EXERCISE

My very first job as a high school junior in 1991 was at a small, women's gym in Wichita called Fitness for Her. I only remember two things really, the first being my boss, Venus, who wore spandex bike shorts under a thong leotard every single day as her work uniform, which was understandably stressful for me to navigate on the regular. I wanted to not see her spandex cheeks sandwiching the thong, but how could one not? I'll answer that: one sees.

The other thing I remember is learning to teach my first step aerobics class. Do people still do step aerobics? Well, in 1991, step class was the shiz and everyone was having it. *Simulate walking up and down stairs? With some jaunty side kicks? Genius!* After receiving around twelve minutes of training, I "taught" my first class, which was an unquestionable disaster.

With no mastery of the language, I'd give instructions like, "Put one foot on the ground and one on the stair, and do your arms kind of like a soldier and we'll do like a march move and in a minute we'll change our feet more like a boxer." *What did this mean?* No one knew, my friends. I didn't even know to lead each step series on the natural four-count; I just started on whatever beat was happening. Think of someone clapping to a song whenever their hands decided to clap instead of on the two and four. I'm pretty sure I caused a few seizures. My step class looked less like an exercise commercial and more like preschool gym time. I'm sure those women were thrilled to pay $49.99 a month to have a sixteen-year-old in Umbros give aerobics instructions by saying "use this hand" and waving it in the air because lefts and rights are hard.

Since 1991, I've had a difficult relationship with working out. I want to love it. I do. I possess a fully developed mental vision of myself as a runner—long strides, fast pace, athletic gait. In reality, I am a lumbering, heavy-footed run-walker whose fingers get swollen after one hundred yards so I hold them upright at a ninety-degree angle, like I am about to clap, resembling Ricky Bobby in *Talladega Nights*: "I don't know what to do with my hands." It is secondhand embarrassing for anyone who must bear witness.

The problem is, I prefer watching Netflix and eating snacks. This is fundamentally superior to sweating and breathing hard. You get to watch shows and arrange your remote controls on one side and your chips and dips on the other. If your cell phone is within reach, you don't even have to get up to parent. You can call your kids from the couch like a true modern mom. This is one million times better than getting a side stitch during Body Pump while breathing in everyone's crotch sweat. I don't even know why I have to explain this.

To be fair, my checkbook communicates that not only do I love exercise, I like to pay for it in monthly bank drafts that are easy to activate but strangely difficult to discontinue, even if, say, you haven't gone to that gym one time in ten and a half months.

The point is, I pay for it like a committed attender, so surely that counts for something. I am helping fund other people's exercise space. You're welcome. My enthusiasm is always concentrated on the front end: *Here! Here! Here, Gold's Gym, Lifetime Fitness, Personal Trainer, Boot Camp Instructor, Fitness Coach, Yoga Master, Nutritional Mentor, Holistic Wellness Practitioner, take my money! Take it! Keep it! Buy some groceries! Pay some bills! Get you something nice! I will use your services for a short amount of time and then not, but please enjoy my money!*

None of this gets easier as you get older, dear reader. Every time I drag my fluffy behind back to the gym, class, or studio, I imagine myself as entirely more fit and capable than I am despite all evidence to the contrary: *Well, let's see, I've been working my sedentary job every day and haven't exercised in fourteen months and ate like it was a paying job this winter and haven't experienced an elevated heart rate since I watched the season finale of* Parenthood, *so . . . I'll take the ninety-minute Bikram hot yoga class because that makes physical and reasonable sense!*

And then I die.

The aging, uncooperative body is one thing, but the gym is a whole 'nother situation. It becomes immediately clear that many people there have been using the membership they paid for. What is this, the Try Hard Convention? Where my sloths at? And of course the treadmills are at the front of the gym with the TVs, so when I haul up there to get my run-walk on, I give everyone a full rear visual assault, and there is no way their membership fees cover that sort of emotional distress. At the height of what I want for my life plan, having fifty people watch me run-walk from behind while my back flesh flaps squeeze out of my sports bra has to be at the top.

And seriously, I've been in (and out of) gyms for twenty-five years, but inevitably I'll approach a weight machine absolutely flummoxed on how to use it. So instead of asking for help like a mature adult, I loosely figure out where the butt, hands, and legs go and just push, pull, squeeze, lift accordingly. Sometimes I am facing the entirely wrong direction. Sometimes, in an effort not to look like a Nancy, I put the weight on the lightest setting, then fall off the machine because pulling with all your might on five pounds tends to unbalance a person. If everyone is looking at me even one-tenth of how much I think they are, I am certainly an unwitting star on YouTube already: "Watch this chubby mom try to use the tricep machine and hit herself in the face and act like nothing happened!"

At this writing, my girlfriends and I are doing hot yoga. Wait, I'm sorry, *practicing* hot yoga. (All yoga is a "practice" and specifically "your own practice," which I take to mean I can lie flat on the mat sometimes because my practice isn't interested in balancing the entire body on one elbow. That is not a thing my practice wants to attempt. Namaste.) Also, I realize it is fundamental to this brand of yoga and is even found right there in the name, but every time we enter the room, one of us says, "Why is it so hot in here?" Then we spend the next hour trying with all our strength not to get the toots or the giggles, but we often get both.

I once thought yoga was for weirdos, but apparently yoga is for hard bodies. I regularly stare at our fellow yogi with wonder because their muscles are a thing to behold. My friends and I watched a girl hold an unsupported handstand in the middle of the room for three minutes yesterday during "inversion practice," which we interpreted as lying on our backs and "inverting" our legs up the wall. *It was what our practices desired.* What grown adult can hold a handstand for three minutes? A sorcerer? Every muscle in her body was defined, and we wondered out loud if we had all the same muscles in our mom bodies because we'd never seen most of them. We want to win the Bicep Contest like her, not the Front Butt Contest we are currently winning in our pants. On our third yoga class, I asked our instructor: "How long until we look like you? Because this is already our third time and I have some expectations."

That is another thing I do. I may go a year and a half with no physical activity, incurring all the pounds and squishy flesh that laziness provides in eighteen months, but after logging four hours of exercise, I expect to fit back into my jeans from last year. I actually try them on after going to the gym three times and weigh myself, anticipating a different second number. I always want a prize for going back, and I want that prize to be a cheerleader's body after a week of classes, regularly shocked that even with seven days in the gym, I still look like a person who types for a living and also loves chips. What is this horse-crappery? After thirty days, I am ready to quit because obviously exercise doesn't work. I didn't lose twenty-five pounds yet, so it will clearly never happen, and I am convinced beyond measure that it is my thyroid.

Anyway, these are my exercise feelings and I don't see them changing anytime soon or ever. I will just never be that girl who "can't wait to get into the gym today" or go for "a quick run." These are not things I will say or feel or mean or do. But I will keep dragging myself back in after another inevitable hiatus, shocked all over again at what inertia does to a forty-two-year-old container, and at the bare minimum, I will wrangle material out of it because I may not *lose* twenty pounds but I can sure write about *wanting to*.

How about some healthy recipes to accompany your work-out phase? I love crap food as much as *anyone*, but even I am loath to pack on five times the calories I just burned going face-down in a bowl of chips and queso like Cookie Monster. Here are three absolutely delicious smoothie recipes that are super good for you and don't taste like sadness and broken dreams. So many ingredients can live for ages in your freezer that you can be ready to rock a smoothie almost constantly. These are awesome for breakfast, midafternoon snack, postworkout refuel, or straight-up dessert.

SMOOTHIES

Let me say this first: I did it. I bought the Vitamix. I plunked down whatever-the-heck dumb amount they asked for and literally drank their Kool-Aid. The thing is, the Hatmakers *drink us some smoothies*, and one of the spawn cannot even deal with a single granule in his drink. Floating bits of kale? Armageddon. And all my Walmart blenders tried their best but ended up in our blender graveyard, so I finally just said, forget it, I'll "invest" (this is how you sell these things to husbands) in a blender that will work forever and if it doesn't, they'll send me a new one. So now you know the story of my blender and thank you for listening. The point is, crappy blenders may or may not give you the smoothie of your dreams without making your house smell like a dumpster fire.

The Green One
This makes four to six smoothies depending on how you pour, so you can cut it in half for sure. It works for us, because my children drink smoothies like they have tapeworms, and even if I'm making this just for me, I like to have several in the fridge to drink for a couple of days. I just pour it in mason jars with lids and hide them behind the pickles so my kids can't see them. Give the jar a quick shake when you pull it out and you are in business.

4 cups baby spinach

4 cups unsweetened coconut milk or almond milk (or real milk because everyone needs to RELAX)

2 oranges, peeled

2 cups cooked sweet potato, chilled (just peel, cube, and steam in the microwave and keep a baggie in your freezer for your smoothie needs)

2 cups chopped frozen pineapple

1 (1-inch) piece fresh ginger, peeled and chopped (I always keep a big, gangly looking ginger root in my freezer and just lob off a piece when I need it)

Juice of 1 lime

Drizzle of honey

Big spoonful of protein powder (order online!)

Blend the spinach and milk first, because spinach is on a mission to jack all manufactured blenders. Get that nice and smooth and then add everything else. If you have a son like mine, put it on top speed and blend for two or three minutes so there will be "no gross floaties in it."

The Peanut Butter and Banana One

Again, you'll get around four smoothies out of these quantities. Halve the recipe if you aren't raising a small army.

4 cups coconut milk, almond milk, or cow's milk

2 cups baby spinach

3 to 4 frozen bananas (we let bunches go brown every week, peel and halve them, and bag them in the freezer)

1 cup unsweetened plain Greek yogurt (or regular
    yogurt; Greek is just nice and thick)
½ cup peanut butter
2 tablespoons Nutella

Blend the milk and spinach until smooth. Add the bananas and blend. Don't freak out if your blender sounds like it is giving birth. Frozen bananas are no joke. Add everything else and blend until it is a creamy gift from God's angels.

The Berry Vanilla One

This also makes around three or four smoothies. We maybe pour a lot. Maybe this makes six where you live. I can't know. Four of my five kids are teenagers right now, and it is like living with Olympic swimmers who have to eat 12,000 calories a day.

1 cup frozen unsweetened raspberries
1 cup frozen unsweetened strawberries
1½ cups unsweetened pineapple juice
2 cups vanilla yogurt

Put it all in your blender and give it a whirl. If this is too tart for you, add a drizzle of honey. Yum.

One of the *luckiest*
things that can
happen to you in life
is, I think, to have a
happy childhood.[1]

–Agatha Christie

CHAPTER 14

THE CABIN

In 1971, Grandma and Grandpa King were leaving Denver to drive home to Kansas after a court reporter convention (my grandpa was the court reporter for *Brown v. Board of Education*), and they saw a sign for a brand-new development near Woodland Park: "Now selling lots in Indian Creek Wilderness Estates," an impressive name that played fast and loose since they didn't even have *electricity*. I don't know many "estates" that run on propane tanks and a generator, but there I go, being all fancy. Anyhow, my grandpa pulled off the highway, drove right to the office, and asked for a lot at the top of a mountain. On the spot, he bought seven acres with a view of Pikes Peak and then built a modified A-frame cabin for $21,000.

The cabin was monumental to my entire childhood.

My siblings, our cousins, and I grew up there and in every neighboring restaurant, store, amusement park (The North Pole!), and back road. In fact, my parents drove to the cabin from Kansas when I was a newborn in winter 1974, and at a restaurant in nearby Florissant, the waitresses asked if they could hold me while my parents ate, since Mom and Dad were one of two couples in the entire place during the off-season and the waitresses didn't have a lot of tables to tend. They spent the next hour walking me around and apparently taking me back to the kitchen, which was not a thing first-time parents concerned themselves about in the seventies.

To paint a picture of the cabin, you first have to know my grandparents. They were quite posh. (Y'all, my grandma passed away at ninety-four a few years ago, and she had her nails done four days before she died. She couldn't walk and could barely move, but heck if she was going to be delivered into the arms of Jesus with grown-out acrylics.) If something was stylish, gaudy, or flashy, my grandma possessed it. Do you think a full-length mink coat just buys itself? No, it does not. And my grandpa regularly walked around with a boss fedora, casually smoking filtered Winstons like something out of a swanky Pan Am ad.

So any cabin of theirs built in 1971 was going to be awash in the current style: it had the thickest red shag carpeting probably ever invented. It looked like the entire floor was covered in Muppets. The kitchen was decked out with avocado-colored appliances and bright-red Formica that did not even mess around. The mid-century modern furniture game was strong: blond wood, skinny metal legs, low and lean cabinets, tufted curved sectional. The console TV was on a mirrored brass beverage cart, because obviously. The cabin was three levels with a huge wraparound cedar deck. The top floor had slanted walls, and we're pretty sure the bottom level was haunted.

It was the cabin of our dreams.

It was the scene of every fourth childhood memory. My parents' tribe often came, too, so my friends share all the same memories. The cabin was in our family for twenty-two years, and during that time, we drove there at least once a year from wherever we lived: Wichita, Kansas; Fort Worth, Texas; Little Rock, Arkansas; Houma, Louisiana. We were a middle-class family that didn't take fancy vacations, so the cabin was our escape, our shared obsession, our summer thrill.

One time we attempted the thirty-six-hour drive from south Louisiana in our 1972 VW van in the dead of winter, and it broke down three times, stranding us in Sharon Springs, Kansas (population 738), where the locals kept visiting the garage to take "that nice family with the unfortunate van" to eat at the diner. We prayed for its recovery because it was truly a van fit for legend and lore. Who wouldn't have wanted this ride: Dad took out the middle seat, cut a piece of carpet to fit, and we spread out sleeping bags and books like we were having a slumber party instead of hurtling down an icy highway unsecured. The only downside, besides imminent physical danger, was how our crayons would melt from the scorching engine a mere four inches away from our sprawled bodies. (My brother doesn't remember this, because he was just a baby in a Moses basket wedged under the stick shift. Safety first.)

When we finally made it to the cabin, my grandpa was so upset, he took my dad straight to a dealership to trade in the van for a brand-new gray station wagon that we named The Ghost. How old school is this: my grandpa told the dealer, "This car will be in my son's name. I don't have any money in my main account to cover it, but I'll wire it over when I get back to Kansas." And the dealer shook his hand and let us drive The Ghost off the lot, deeded to one man because some other old guy promised to pay for it later. He simply asked my dad: "Could you ship me that middle seat sometime?" It was the nicest car we'd ever owned.

The Ghost was an accomplice in one of our favorite cabin memories. My brother Drew and cousin Dori asked to watch a movie in The Ghost, because our only VCR plugged into a car lighter. They were six and seven years old respectively, and I have no idea how to help you process this, but the movie our parents allowed two first graders to watch inside a parked station wagon in the woods in the black of night was *Candyman*, an R-rated horror movie that made grown adults flee the theater.

This outrageous parenting decision from yesteryear was bad enough, but my dad and uncle snuck out the back door of the cabin, counted to three, then banged on the car windows and screamed to further traumatize their youngest children who had just learned to read. To this living day, Drew and Dori break out in cold sweats at the memory and refuse to watch scary movies. It never even occurred to Dad and Uncle Tom to feel bad, because those were not the days of parent guilt, my friends.

My grandparents' best friends, Ann and Hoppy, built a cabin right across the street, and by "street" I mean the one-lane gravel road that precariously snaked up the mountain to the "estates" (we had to pull off the road to let oncoming cars pass). Virtually every day, we'd trek across the crunchy street to pitch horseshoes with Hoppy and drink Ann's Tab after Grandma cut us off. They would come to our cabin at night and play Chicken Foot and 42 with us for hours. Nothing said "I am a child of the seventies" like having grandparents who taught you dominos on their lacquered table while drinking Sanka.

Our parents basically let us have the run of the mountain in those days. We spent 80 percent of every day outside scrambling up boulders, riding our bikes, climbing trees, and making up "programs," which we inflicted on our parents with no restraint or mercy. As the oldest cousin, I was always the director and everyone else my subjects. The programs were endless and complicated, and to this day I can still conjure the barely suppressed rage when none of those fools followed my choreography correctly: *Lindsay, raise the umbrella and say your line! GAH!* One time we held a beauty pageant in which I was the director, Lindsay and Angie were the emcees, and Cortney and Dori were the only contestants. They dressed up in sheets. Dori won and Cortney got Miss Congeniality, for which she is still enraged. (Seriously, get some counseling.) Our parents tried to pull the *we'll just turn the TV down during the program*, but we weren't having it. *TV off, jokers. We've been practicing for six hours.*

The cabin encapsulated the magic of childhood. Every year, we'd build another layer of memories, adding to the growing monument of our family story. Even now, a smell, a sound, even just a key word sends us deep diving into the stored vault of twenty-two years out there together. The enchantment is all certainly inflated in memory, as these things often are, much like when you return to your childhood home and find it impossibly shrunk, but the cabin years provided touchstones for family solidarity into adulthood: this is what we did, this is where we went, this is how we laughed, this is what we shared.

Mamas, the traditions and experiences we provide during the Family Years are paving a road our kids can always return to, one that always points home. There is something about a recurring shared memory; the sum becomes greater than the parts.

Childhood is such a wonky, weird season. Do you remember the fears and confusion and insecurities we harbored, our own little private pile of worries? Kids are amazingly resilient and handle change better than we give them credit for, but there is something to be said for a given, some constant, an element of childhood that delivers over and over with predictability and joy. While their bodies and minds and friends and classes are a swirling vortex of volatility, while they are constantly required to adjust and shift and recalibrate and flex, providing a familiar touchpoint week after week or year after year is an anchor that keeps them grounded and a buffer against the scary winds of change. It says to them: *Yes, everything is fluctuating, but you can count on this thing we do, this place we go, this meal we share, this memory we make.*

None of this needs to be expensive or fancy. Nor does it have to be incredibly comprehensive. I heard a speaker at a Christmas brunch once give a talk on traditions, and hand to God, she described *at least fifty traditions* she provided for her children: daily lunch notes with hand-drawn cartoons, thirty Birthday Month activities, leaving surprises under the lining of their trash cans to discover upon weekly removal, the What We Learned Today journal, family time capsules, the weekly thankful box. I don't think there was one day of the year that didn't involve some meaningful moment. I basically did a slow slide out of my chair onto the ground, because LADY PLEASE, I AM JUST TRYING NOT TO MAKE MAC AND CHEESE FOUR NIGHTS A WEEK.

Traditions can be simple. Heck, my girlfriend's grown kids never stop talking about Friday Puzzle Night. It can be anything: Saturday pancakes and bacon, that rental house in Destin, Monopoly Monday, cutting down a Christmas tree together, lake days, sledding down that one hill every year, family camp, Grandma's house, summer road trips, popcorn and movie night, backyard picnics. Whether it is a place you return to, a tradition you create, or a story you rewrite over and over together, miraculously, the fighting and whining and eye-rolling that often accompany that custom will one day recede and what emerges is a rock-solid bank of memories your family will share forever. Never fear, Mamas, the energy you are logging toward any tradition will not return void. You are building something special, and your kids will not forget.

I know I didn't. I *remembered.*

And then one day, say, twenty-three years after your special place is gone, one of your grown kids might call your family together on your back porch because she wants to write about this tradition and mine everyone's memories, and your husband will walk out with his outdated camcorder to record the conversation that is supposed to last around thirty minutes but goes on for three hours, because once you start down the rabbit hole of VW vans and haunted basements and programs and Chicken Foot, your laughter carries you from one memory to the next, and that grown daughter will finally tell her sister to just open another bottle of wine because, happily, you are all going to be there for quite a while.

I used to be

Snow White,

but I drifted.[1]

–MAE WEST

CHAPTER 15

DOLDRUMS

Author's note: This essay does not apply to serious trauma or depression. The doldrums are a funk, not a severe crisis. Sometimes we require therapy, intervention, and possibly medication, and the practices I describe are inadequate.

dol·drums
[dohl-dru*h* mz, dol-, dawl-]
noun (used with a plural verb)
    1. a state of inactivity or stagnation, as in business or art: *August is a time of doldrums for many enterprises.*
    2. a belt of calms and light baffling winds north of the equator between the northern and southern trade winds in the Atlantic and Pacific oceans.
    3. a dull, listless, depressed mood; low spirits.[1]

Conversation with Brandon:

> ME: Blah.
> B: What's wrong?
> ME: Nothing. Just everything. Everything is bad.

B: Specifically?

ME: Just that our kids are probably all going to hate us and struggle with multiple incarcerations, I apparently will gain a pound a month until I die, this house is a craphole of chaos, and my weird quirks are getting worse. I hid in the bathroom at another conference.

B: Is that all?

ME: And also, only two of my kids love to read, so obviously, *Failure, your name is Motherhood*, and all I do is discipline and put out fires, so I've basically come to hate the sound of my own voice. I can't stand myself, and these kids aren't faring much better on my Like-O-Meter. And I'm sorry to tell you, but your scores aren't great either. I cannot even talk about e-mails. My Bible feels like a useless lead weight. I don't feel like I'm taking skin care seriously enough. I also ate a tub of pimento cheese. All hope is lost.

B: But at least you're working on that melodramatic tendency.

ME: Just lost another four points, pal. Feels like a dangerous time to mess with me.

I essentially slid into a two-month case of the doldrums, trapped by inertia and overwhelmed by the escape requirements. On my best days, our life is heavy duty, but during my low days, I Google search "fake my own death and disappear," which Brandon might dub melodramatic, but he is just a man with a stable mind and can't be trusted.

Here is the bummer about the doldrums: the very efforts needed to lift yourself out are the same things you've lost energy to do. The simplest remedies feel like weights drudged up from the bottom of the ocean. Your mind knows to do them, but your will refuses to cooperate. Which makes your mind furious and mired in shame, which makes your will dig its heels and wallow, which makes you realize you are turning on yourself. You are your own worst enemy. No one can oppress me like myself.

How did I eventually get out of this funk? Nothing miraculous happened, except one day I said, *This is enough.* Virtually nothing changed that day. Or the next. These things aren't overnight success stories, because if it took three months and 459 lazy, unhealthy choices to get stuck, it takes some time to climb out. Also, the work required is unsexy, ordinary, boring old labor that lacks the appeal of instant gratification and the pizzazz of an unsolicited miracle. I wish I had better news about breaking free, but apparently we just have to grab a shovel and start digging.

Dear one, if you are stuck in the doldrums—and may I say that I love you and you are not alone—let me offer up some of the labors that pulled me through, one teeny moment at a time.

First, I made a list of everything I was behind on. Unfinished tasks are a cloud of doom over my head. The emotional energy they steal from me is unbearable. So I wrote them down to get a handle on them rather than leave them floating around unnamed, unmanaged, unidentified. It was ironic, because each line item could be accomplished in minutes at best, a day at worst: mail these things, return this, make those appointments, answer these e-mails (deliver me, Lord), scan over that contract, send in money for that school thing (this times a zillion, free public school my eye), pick up that stuff, return that phone call, finish writing that article. Overdue responsibilities contribute heavily to my shame spiral, and writing them down and slowly crossing them off was an instant boon, literally. Unbelievable the weight that rolls off when the Behind Pile starts to shrink.

Second, the house. For the love of Oprah, the house. I am one of those annoying people who requires tidiness and declutterfication. Oh, to peacefully live in chaos among the piles instead of, hypothetically, barking at the humans who live with me and begrudging everyone for being such slobs. But nope. That is not my lot in life. A cluttered, disorganized house has a direct correlation to my cluttered, disorganized mind.

So, brace yourselves, we launched another chore chart. (I know. Matter of time. I am *drawn* to systems but struggle to *maintain* them.) But this one was simple and repetitive: Everyone had one chore a day, and it was the same every week. This was not for pay, because the reward was getting to live in my house for free. The kids had done these tasks before but with no regularity and primarily after I turned into a lunatic. Now we had formalized it somewhat, and the house-maintaining was more consistent. Not allowing our abode to slip into entropy was mentally healing. The chart may be imperfect, but even loose structure restores order to my inner turmoil. Simply creating a plan provides some dignity, which is a powerful combatant to the doldrums.

Third, parenting. Obviously my five kids are perfect and make straight As and speak loving words to each other constantly, but clearly their classmates had poorly influenced them, because they turned into maniacs. This surely had nothing to do with their mother's two-month doldrum disorder, because children are never the thermometer simply displaying the temperature of their parents. I'm sure their digression was just a coincidence.

So anyway, this thing happened where the kids were horrible and fighting and I went to my room to cry about these terrible children God stuck me with, and He immediately brought to mind six—*six*—lovely moments my kids had engineered that very day and I heard, "You are only noticing the bad moments and ignoring the good ones."

God never coddles me when I want Him to. It's infuriating.

So we started the Brag Board. (It's just a chalkboard, but can we give a quick shout-out to the Chalkboard Paint People for completely rebranding and becoming the darling of Pinterest? I mean, there were chalkboards on *Little House on the Prairie*. They aren't new is all I'm saying.) Anytime we catch someone being kind, helpful, gracious, or awesome, we write it down, big or small. It has to be about someone else, because my offspring would write: *It was so incredible how I unloaded the dishwasher.*

Funny thing: I'm not positive they've had more shining moments lately than before, but I'm sure noticing them now. Evidently we will see exactly what we're looking for. Does this mean I've had to follow a kid or two around, searching for one tiny good thing to say? Yep. But catching children in their goodness totally beats reprimanding them only in their struggles, and the Brag Board pulled the whole family up a few degrees.

Finally, I made a list of all the practices that make me feel healthy. Not surprisingly, I noticed most were absent in my doldrums: cooking, reading good books, limiting screen time, eating well, date nights, taking walks, scheduling time with a counselor, being outside, praying, changing out of my pajamas (this is a thing for work-at-homes), spending time with my friends. All ordinary, nothing new or dramatic. These are mainly bits and pieces that fit in the gaps of life. I simply committed some time back to my staples, maybe just one a day.

None of these were executed immediately. Over a few weeks, I slowly implemented healthier practices, one at a time. It was not revolutionary to sit down with Alan Bradley's latest novel (*"Whenever I'm a little blue I think about cyanide, which so perfectly reflects my mood."—Flavia*), nor was the world righted after the first entry on the Brag Board. The chore chart didn't solve the crisis, and neither did catching up on e-mails.

But all together, over weeks, just doing the work, bit by bit, digging deep for diligence and grace and best practices, the doldrums receded. These measures make us healthy and whole, because we stop succumbing to disorder and shame. It's not fancy or quick work, unfortunately, but it is effective.

If you feel stuck today, can I suggest approaching the doldrums in a reasonable way, one tiny element at a time? Alone, none are monumental, but together they lay small paver stones out of the mire, forging a path back to health, back to vibrancy. It will be imperfect with incremental steps forward and back, but God can use your brave movement to soothe the shame of stagnation and restore peace to the chaos.

How about an easy little recipe to get you started? I am not even kidding when I say that making a delicious dish with your hands and enjoying it with your mouth is really something. It is a small rung to higher ground. Do not say to yourself, *This is one more thing I can't pull off*, but rather, *This is one easy thing I can accomplish in fifteen minutes.* This is guaranteed to improve your spirits, if only in the consumption.

A few months ago, we were invited to Willie and Korie Robertson's house for a long weekend (Korie and I traveled to Ethiopia together to raise money for vulnerable families through Help One Now, and we bonded during our daily traumatic van marathons—see chapter 3). Korie's aunt hosts enormous Sunday lunches after church, and we finagled an invite. There I was, putting a bunch of southern food on my plate, and oh fine, I guess I'll throw this salad on here to be nice.

Jen eats bite of salad

Jen's life is changed

JEN: Um, who made this salad? What is this salad?

KORIE: Oh, that's Aunt Carol's Crunchy Salad. We make her bring it to every meal.

JEN: Which one is Aunt Carol?

(Conversation gets sidetracked)

JEN: Uh-huh. Yeah. Anyway, who is Aunt Carol?

(Some random pointing in the other room)

JEN: Which one?

(Some vague describing)
(Conversation moves on)
(Jen gets up and goes into the other room)

JEN: Excuse me for interrupting. I need to speak to whichever one of you is Aunt Carol.

I badgered her for the recipe, and here it is. And just in case you are thinking, *Great, Jen. I have the doldrums, and you are feeding me salad?* just trust me. I am not playing. This is magical salad.

Aunt Carol's Crunchy Salad

Salad

    2 tablespoons butter

    1 package ramen noodles (like the $.13 package)

    1/2 cup or so of chopped almonds

    Handful of sunflower seeds

    4 to 6 cups sturdy lettuce (I like romaine)

2 cups or so of chopped broccoli
Some chopped green onions
You can add any crunchy thing: carrots, radishes,
    snap peas, cabbage

Melt the butter in a skillet over medium-high heat. Add the uncooked ramen noodles (break them all up), almonds, and sunflower seeds, and saute until toasted light brown. Maybe 3 to 4 minutes. Let cool.

Pour the dressing (recipe below) into the bottom of your salad bowl.

Add the lettuce, broccoli, green onions, and toasted crunch mix. Toss when ready to serve.

Vinaigrette

4 tablespoons brown sugar
1 teaspoon salt
6 tablespoons rice wine vinegar
2 to 3 drops Tabasco
½ cup oil (olive, sunflower, walnut, whatever oil you
    like. Aunt Carol uses canola oil, so no need to get
    trendy)

Mix all the vinaigrette ingredients with a whisk (or just shake this all together in a mason jar if you want to control the quantity or make extra).

This is so good. Cannot deal. Add chicken or shrimp, and it is a whole meal. This is a doldrum fixer. I'm so serious. Aunt Carol and I are here for you.

Related: I think Aunt Carol solved my issue with kale. The last time I made this, I chopped kale in bite-sized pieces and tossed it with the romaine and all the other goodies plus *the dressing* (which I could drink with a straw). It is the only time I have ever had kind feelings toward kale.

Don't talk to me about it, Kale Propaganda People. Stop trying to convert us. I know all the things. I still don't like it. *Except slathered in Aunt Carol's dressing.*

Football is, after all,
a wonderful way
to get *rid* of your
aggressions without
going to jail for it.[1]

–HEYWOOD HALE BROUN

CHAPTER 16

IDENTIFIABLE SIGNS OF ATHLETIC GREATNESS

f it is possible to feel both judgmental about something ridiculous while at the same time fully participating in its jackassery, that is my complicity in Southern Football.

For southerners, sure, there are baseball and soccer. We have basketball and swimming like everyone else. But those are small planets orbiting the blazing sun of football. It is king and everyone else its subjects. The president of the University of Texas makes in seven years what the football coach makes in one season; add post-season bonuses, and the differential stretches out till, basically, infinity. Educate our state's young adults? Sure, I guess, whatever. Serve up two losing football seasons in a row? BYE, FELICIA.

For us, the path to the NFL begins in prekindergarten when dads and moms alike begin to assess their sons for identifiable signs of athletic greatness. Never mind that he still wets the bed; the question is, *Does he possess the hand girth to throw a tight spiral?* With complete sincerity, parents defend the decision to enroll their glorified toddler in a competitive flag football league, because if they wait until second grade, "it is too late." Obviously, at that point, he will be hopelessly behind the other boys who are just learning to subtract but can already run eleven defensive plays. (In case you are wondering where I fall on the "judge or participate" spectrum, perhaps I can show you this adorable picture of my five-year-old in football pads.)

It's serious business, you guys. For every junior team, you will find a corresponding sea of parents in matching jerseys, hats, buttons, and hoodies. They will be rattling homemade shakers and waving matching pom-poms. There will be team moms, team snacks, team e-mails, team tents, team chants, team cheerleading squads, team signs, team fund-raisers, team merch, and team hysteria. So completely over-the-top is the system, an outsider would suspect it was fake, like a made-for-TV Disney movie in which an overzealous youth league is caught rigging birth certificates so middle schoolers can play in the Under 8 Division.

Our son Ben plays competitive youth football, and his team has given up six points in two years. He practices three nights a week, including one night devoted to *Blu-ray game film* from the week before (Jesus, be my strength). Six adult men coach his team, and they are as serious as Vladimir Putin. Ben has not one but two Kid-Sized Super Bowl rings, because this is a thing southern parents spend their cash money on to demonstrate athletic triumph.

These children still have Valentine's Day parties at school.

Our fields have bleachers, but they are utilized only by attending grandmas and grandpas (of which they are legion). Moms and dads don't require bleachers, because they stand at the fence and "help coach." I'm sure this is a delight to the coaches. Dads are sure to yell alternative advice in case the play calls don't showcase their sons' particular skill sets. Before games, I've overheard many boys beg dads not to bellow instructions from the fence, at which point the dads promise they will not, which is an outright lie. In addition to sideline play calling, they are also useful for screaming out Obvious Commands: *Hustle! Run fast! Block your man! Score!*

Thanks, dads.

But they have nothing on the moms. This is where the train goes entirely off the tracks. I'm sure Football Moms act perfectly ordinary in their workplaces or at the mall or church. But you put their baby boys out on a football field as middle linebackers, and every bit of crazy they have been repressing all week comes out in full explosion. I've heard the following words screeched by FMs at top volume:

Zachary, hit him with all your might, son!

Ty, you better not let him past you, or you'll answer for it!

Juan, put your shoulder down and block like a man!

I don't know what the parenting books would say about this, but I think it's safe to say this approach is off the grid. Football Moms—we simultaneously wield a wide-angle camera, spirit shaker, air horn, and terrifying aggression. And by "we" I mean "me," because one time the referee got me so turnt, I waited for him at his car like a serial killer and demanded an explanation for his particular level of incompetence. (I need mentorship to check my life.)

None of this improves as the kids get older. High school football in the South is so intense a whole TV series was crafted after it starring dreamy Taylor Kitsch as Tim Riggins, which promptly put me into Thought Prison, because I wasn't sure if I should be his girlfriend or his mother. Anyhow, *Clear Eyes, Full Hearts, Can't Lose* is basically the southern mantra, and *Friday Night Lights* just made it public. Now you know our old men sit in coffee shops and discuss ways to torment new coaches and underperforming athletic directors.

In the past decade, more than 50 percent of the top draft picks in the NFL were southern high school boys who had attended sleep-away quarterback camps since they were in fifth grade. There never has been and never will be any of that "we're all winners" crap down here. Pretty sure "participation trophies" are melted down and refashioned into a statue of Denzel Washington's character from *Remember the Titans*. In top divisions, highly ranked high school players are recruited and moved into elite school districts to secure state championships, and this is why the South is the most ridiculous region in these United States of America.

All this really just sets the stage for the Big Enchilada: college football. If you haven't seen a grown man wear a Mississippi State T-shirt to a business meeting with zero self-consciousness, then you must live in Alaska or New Hampshire, or somewhere people don't wear university gear as business casual attire though they graduated from college twenty-seven years ago. After all, receiving your college diploma is really just the start of your Adult Allegiance Program; there are rules, clubs, specialty bars, lingo, gear, handshakes, donor funds, loyalty programs, alumni meet-ups, and a deep well of hostility toward rivals the rest of your living life.

All our children learned "The Eyes of Texas" as part of their public school kindergarten curriculum. My friend Becky's daughter—from a dyed-in-the-wool Texas A&M family—came home from kindergarten hysterically crying after the UT song indoctrination: "Daddy is going to be so mad at me!" My friend Jenny's dad had a bona fide low-grade heart attack during a University of Alabama playoff game. Not one but eight of my friends named their children and pets after college stadiums. We scheduled an anniversary trip to Europe around a Longhorn away game.

I'm just saying we probably all need some psychoanalysis.

The obvious irony is that after all this hysteria, almost none of our sons will actually play college football, much less secure a spot in the NFL. (I *knew* we should have started him in first grade instead of third!) Sure, only 6.5 percent of high school athletes will play college football, and only 1.5 percent of college players will move on to the pros, but *we pray before our public school games*, so we're playing with the Lord's favor, and I'm pretty sure the Savior wants my son to receive a full ride for his outstanding performance as tight end.

Anyhow, it mostly boils down to a bunch of middle-aged people wearing school colors and cheering for the team they've loved since 1989. The end game for most of us is perfecting our tailgate parties. (Brandon and I built a huge porch on our old house last year, and upon seeing it, 100 percent of our friends said, "This is perfect for watching football." Obviously. Why even have a porch if there is no TV on it for playoffs? We're not amateurs.)

So for all my fellow football lunatics, here are a couple of no-fail recipes for your watch parties or tailgate crews. And listen, no one said football food was supposed to be healthy, okay? It is simply understood that game day recipes can involve a disproportionate amount of mayonnaise, cheese, red meat, or TTAF (things that are fried). Don't hate the playa, hate the game.

BUFFALO CHICKEN DIP

My girlfriend Tonya first introduced me to this winner, and I have never had an ounce of leftovers. Not even enough for one bloomin' chip. It is so easy, I don't even know if we can call it a recipe, but you know what we can call it? A PARTY IN OUR MOUTHS.

1 (8-ounce) block cream cheese, softened
3 cups cooked, shredded chicken (I always buy the grocery store rotisserie bird)
1 cup buffalo wing sauce (any kind you like)
1 cup blue cheese dressing*
1 (8-ounce) tub blue cheese crumbles (if you're scared, use Cheddar, but COME ON, BRO)

Options for dippers: chips, crackers, celery sticks, crostini, slider rolls, *whatever man.*

Preheat the oven to 350 degrees. Spread the softened cream cheese in the bottom of a square baking dish. In a bowl, mix the shredded chicken with the wing sauce and blue cheese dressing until completely coated. Spread the chicken mixture evenly on top of the cream cheese. Top with the blue cheese crumbles. Warm through for around ten minutes (you don't want to cook this too long because the cream cheese gets melted and runny, and that is no way to live).

Pile up any dipper you want.

This is spicy and creamy, and it literally got me through the 2010 National Championship game when Colt McCoy got injured on the fifth play and we handed off our dreams to a freshman quarterback who had ridden the pine since August. The only winner that day was the buffalo dip, my friends.

* If you hate blue cheese, you can substitute ranch dressing here, but in that case, perhaps you should give this recipe a new name because the only thing worse than serving your friends something called "Buffalo Chicken Dip" without blue cheese is stocking your cooler with O'Doul's. It's un-American.

BACON-WRAPPED STUFFED DATES

I cannot even with these. I cannot even, and I cannot odd. I actually think these are a sin. I'm sorry, Lord, but I need these in my mouth. And may I bless with heavenly blessings the first pioneer who decided to make cheese out of a mama goat's lactation. The following quantities make about a pan full, but by all means, double this bad boy if you're feeding a big crew.

1-pound tub pitted dates
1-pound package bacon, cut in half or thirds (not thick-
    cut bacon)
4-ounce log fresh goat cheese or cream cheese
6 ounces roasted almonds
Balsamic reduction*

Preheat the oven to 350 degrees. Use a paring knife to make a slit on one side of each date, but don't cut all the way through. Pitted dates are kind of hollow inside, because they obviously want to be filled with almonds and goat cheese. If your dates have the pits inside, just remove them after you cut the slits. It is their culinary destiny. Fill each date with a bit of goat cheese and one almond, close it, and wrap the whole thing with half a strip of bacon. Place on a baking sheet seam down (don't crowd the pan), and bake for 20 to 30 minutes until the bacon is nice and brown.

These can be served at room temperature (make before!) drizzled with balsamic reduction. They are sweet and salty and creamy and crunchy and chewy, and you almost feel like you should go to confession after eating one. Forgive us, Lord, but there was bacon.

*You already have balsamic reduction in your fridge if you have paid any attention to me online. It's something you need to have. If you, for some reason, do not have it, make some stat! Heat 3 to 4 cups of balsamic vinegar plus 1 tablespoon of sugar in a saucepan over medium heat until it reduces by half and looks like syrup (if it coats the back of a spoon, it's ready). It is sweet and basically perfect. Store in a closed container (I use a mason jar) and keep it in your fridge. Drizzle it on everything (veggies, potatoes, eggs, ice cream, strawberries, avocados, salad, chicken, salmon, pasta, cheese and crackers, air).

Any time women come together with a collective intention, it's a *powerful* thing. Whether it's sitting down making a quilt, in a kitchen preparing a meal, in a club reading the same book, or around the table playing cards, or planning a birthday party, when *women* come *together* with a collective intention, *magic* happens.[1]

–PHYLICIA RASHAD

CHAPTER 17

BONUS MOMS

Last summer, as often happens, the Hatmaker Moving Parts outpaced our bandwidth, and we had to call in reinforcements. (We have five kids, and they mostly all live here and it is just bananas, you guys.) So my friend Amy took Ben for a couple of days while we shuttled other kids somewhere or flew somewhere or whatever cluster we were managing.

Amy is a rare find. I have never seen her remotely unhinged, *and she homeschools four sons* in the house her husband grew up in. She manages this Zen because she quietly, gently curses like a sailor and fancies bourbon. She is always sending articles about weird stuff like emu oil and protein structures of different mammalian milks and how Thomas Jefferson wasn't math educated until thirteen. She once took a maimed chicken to the vet instead of the dinner table. When the flu struck our house last year, she called in $150 worth of holistic oils and colloidal silver and lauric acid to our hippie pharmacy with explicit instructions, and I proceeded to pump my people full of crazy for the next week. (Fine, the flu was totally eradicated.) Amy once locked me into a discussion on "sacred geometry on the micro and macro levels," so that probably explains things well enough.

I tell you all this so you can make sense of her text to me during Ben's stay:

"Burying dead parakeet at 10:15 p.m. in the backyard, and Ben dug up old cat bones. I think. Not sure. Have buried 20 animals back there since 1976. We all had on headlamps. Changed hole locations and went on with ceremony. Might be traumatized. Be aware."

This is what happens when your granola, unschooling, earth mama friend lives in a pet cemetery: your son becomes a grave-digger and has attended not one but two services for Amy's dead animals. (Tiffany, the handlebar-riding chicken, began resurfacing after a few months and required a second ceremony and bigger rocks. Ride or die, Tiffany.)

Jenny, Shonna, Stephanie, Trina, Michelle, Tonya, Alison, Angie, Lana, Lindsay, Cortney, Sarah, Amy: these girls are the ones I lovingly refer to as my kids' Bonus Moms. Some go back to my oldest in diapers, some in the last five years, but all have stood in as extra mothers to my children, and me to theirs.

From my earliest memory, Bonus Moms were a given, a childhood staple. Sure, I was raised by Jana King, but I was also parented by Sharon, Melissa, Prissy, Cheryl, Judy, Rita, and Debbie. I knew their houses as well as my own, and their kids were practically my brothers and sisters. I was either grounded or swatted by each and every one of them, and I have nearly as many memories under their care as my own parents'. I loved them like an extra daughter, and their faces were in all our pictures: vacations, games, graduations, weddings, baby showers.

Because my mom assembled such a tight tribe, I had a precedent for prioritizing my own, my girlfriends, my consortium of Bonus Moms. At first, it was simply survival, as early childhood often is. In that stage, it seems like every friend is having a baby every five minutes, and when you get together, you *must* group-parent or someone might not make it out alive. To this day, I cannot believe my girlfriends and I met at the pool with almost twenty children under five between us. We'd set up watch stations around the perimeter and chatter across the pool while pulling one anothers' toddlers out of the water periodically, dabbing more sunscreen on any kid in reach. We'd group feed them with whatever we scavenged from our kitchens: six peanut butter and jelly sandwiches (one on inside-out end pieces of bread), five pieces of leftover pizza, two bags of Goldfish crackers, some grapes on their last legs, three baggies of carrots, and eight juice boxes. It was like the loaves and fishes—somehow it always stretched.

In the preschool years, the Bonus Moms traded kids and swapped free days. Trina and I rotated: Tuesdays at my house and Thursdays at hers. Six straight hours of liberty to grocery shop and clean toilets was the sort of dream life we'd only read about. Our kids barely had a memory without each other, so parenting three or six? What was the diff? We basically had the same rules, the same food, the same parenting style, and the same naptimes. Our kids were like a tiny pack of wolves, and we raised them as a conglomerate.

Trina's youngest daughter Hannah and my Gavin were absolute best pals and had more sleepovers than I could ever number. (When we moved neighborhoods and ended their future in the same middle and high school, Hannah cried bitter tears and Gavin stopped speaking to us.) Anyhow, Gavin had night terrors until he was six, and during one sleepover with Hannah, he woke up screaming nonsensically about spiders in his bed. Trina's husband, Andrew, quick on the draw, sprinkled baby powder all over Gavin's bunk and declared it "a spider's worst nightmare." We used that trick for the next ten years. (Huge shout-out to Bonus Dads too!)

When my mind wanders back over those years, I cannot recall a single scene that didn't include my girlfriends feeding my kids at their tables, bathing them in their bathtubs, squeezing their ketchup at Chick-fil-A, holding their hands crossing parking lots. I braided their daughters' hair, tucked extra sons into bed, wiped their noses against their wishes, attended their band concerts. Our husbands always group texted us, looking for a specific wife, knowing she was likely among her tribe, or in any case, one of us was probably supervising her kids.

As we got older and parenting became less strenuous physically but more complicated emotionally, Bonus Moms became ever more vital. I once hoped to be the repository of every precious secret, every social apprehension, every burning question my children harbored. But as real life took prominence, much like it did for all of us, I realized teenagers need other trusted adults to help them navigate the pitfalls of adolescence, because some conversations are easier broached with someone Not Mom.

This season introduced a whole new crop of Bonus Moms, some who were not even mothers in the traditional sense of the word. AJ, Shea, Angie, Kelly, Kim, Sam, Faitth: these women became safe havens spiritually, emotionally. A few of them have not yet reached thirty, but they've invested deeply in my children and, consequently, became their confidants, advisors, mentors I trust and love. They connect with my kids at Bible studies and coffee shops, over movies and hiking, Snapchatting and texting. One time, Faitth, twenty-five, asked to spend the day with Sydney, fifteen, and an hour later I received this text: "Can we drive to Fort Worth and get popsicles at Steel City Pops?" This was a three-hour drive from Austin. One way. So my sophomore and this vibrant young adult drove six hours round trip for four popsicles.

If I once imagined this threatening, now I am only pro-foundly grateful my kids have a stable of trusted advisors at the ready. Mamas, we need not become territorial over our chil-dren's every thought and concern. What a gift to surround them with a team of Bonus Moms (and Bonus Dads), trustworthy adults who love our kids and stand available to lead, counsel, basically reinforce everything we've ever said but somehow come off more credible. We want this for them, a safe runway to complicated discussions, a place to warm up, to slowly acceler-ate, to try out ideas before takeoff, if not with us then with other adults we trust.

I rarely hear anyone talk about this, but sometimes a mom simply has a different personality than a kid or two. This obvi-ously isn't about love, affection, or devotion; those are completely intact. It might just be a matter of an extrovert raising an intro-vert, a shy mom raising a rabble-rouser, an academic raising a cowboy, a party planner raising a mathlete. Sometimes, our DNA combines in interesting ways, or we grow our families outside of biology, and we end up parenting a child with a completely differ-ent operating system from how we are wired.

For example, our family is incredibly fluent in sarcasm. Satire is our religion, and we are its disciples. If it is snarky, ironic, hilari-ous, or slightly inappropriate, we are down. Gavin's sixteenth birthday present was live tickets to Jim Gaffigan's comedy show. We share hilarious memes, snarky group texts, stand-up comedy podcasts, and vintage comics.

Except for one little precious family member who came to us at age five. She is a purist, a literal, a tender heart who doesn't understand a solitary word of sarcasm and is regularly horrified, terrified, confused, shocked by our conversations. Upon discover-ing the complete consumption of a twelve-pack of Coke in one night, my husband said at the breakfast table the next morning:

"Guys, I think we've been robbed. A band of thieves must have broken in and stolen all the Cokes."

SONS: Weird. You would think they'd take the TV.
We should report it.
REMY: *What??!! We were robbed????*

It is a hard life for her, this trying to discern sarcasm. While the rest of us bantered in affectionate satire, that poor soul went to school having barely escaped the fresh knowledge that our house was violated by cola bandits. Add to this her love for structure, schedules, and a detailed agenda to the minute, and sometimes it is difficult to understand a sarcastic, loosey-goosey mama who struggles with sensory overload.

No one is right or wrong in the slightest. Just different.

So my friend Michelle is the absolute dearest Bonus Mom for my little one. She provides a secondary environment where all her wonderful traits are understood and celebrated. On Remy's ninth birthday, aware that waiting until 5:00 p.m. for her party would exacerbate her particular anxieties about details and expectations, Michelle drove to my house at 9:00 a.m. and swooped her away for the day as a blessed distraction, delivering her back with five minutes to spare. I didn't even ask for this. She just knew. Because she is an attentive, loving, intuitive Bonus Mom. (Plus, Michelle's husband is Brazilian, which accounts for Remy's obsession with Shakira and her insistence that at *Mrs. Barreto's* house, they are "international." My little Ethiopian also doesn't understand irony.)

Bonus Moms can lend fresh, enthusiastic ears to our children who operate in their personality spheres. My friends readily pass off their budding writers to my counsel, and my girlfriend Tonya takes Ben to Six Flags with her boys every summer (crowded theme parks in July are where all my dreams go to die). Sharing the parenting load with other trusted adults increases our capacity and sustainability. What a gift for our children to know they are deeply loved at another home or two besides their own, that a Bonus Mom or Dad is proud of them and in their corner too. We cannot overlove our children with too many doting adults; there is no such thing as too much adult affection lavished on any kid. Childhood and adolescence comes with such deep insecurity, so many questions and worries about the world and their place in it, providing additional layers of bedrock through Bonus Parents is a buttress, a safety net, a balm.

When my girlfriend Jenny and her family moved to Austin from Corpus Christi to plant our church with us, her children moved from the only home they'd ever known. Her oldest son, easily the nicest, most gentle kid in Texas, was immediately bullied by a *pubescent psychopath* (I'm still bitter). Like, daily taunting, punch-in-the-face bullied. It was devastating and disorienting, and having already sacrificed so much for us and the church, Jenny and I were undone that her son was now suffering even more.

On the face-punch day, Jenny and I went upstairs to his room, crawled on either side of him in his bed, and the three of us cried our eyes out. Just a mom, a Bonus Mom, and an enormous eighth-grade boy bigger than both of us. There was no avoiding us; we were family and I'd once given this big kid more baths than I could count. He was going to suffer our broken hearts. (Especially since our husbands downstairs gave him this exact advice: "Find a corner where no teacher is looking, and take him out. It will only take one time." I'm just saying he received a variety of parental responses.)

Last week I was an accomplice in an elaborate scheme in which that same kid got engaged on a lake trip with all of us and his third Bonus Family. While he got down on one knee, Jenny smiled on lovingly, thrilled but dry-eyed while his two Bonus Moms bawled our ever-blessed eyes out. He was one of our own, one we all raised together, out there with a girl and a ring, growing up despite our threats, while all our other kids and Bonus Kids cheered and took pictures, and we claimed a portion of the day's happiness because we'd logged so many years group parenting and group disciplining and group mentoring and group defending, and by gosh, we were going to celebrate like he was our own flesh and blood. We popped champagne, made toasts, and started planning our first wedding like proper Bonus Mothers-in-Law.

We promise not to be obnoxious.

I mean, we promise to try.

How To
(Part Three)

How to pick a restaurant with your husband or significant other

1. Wait until he asks the fated question, "Where do you want to eat?"
2. Respond with, "Whatever. I'm breezy." Imagine sincerely that you mean this, because you can't think of anywhere specific.
3. Turn down his every suggestion with a grunt, scowl, or dismissive wave of the hand.
4. Become moody and frustrated with his inability to correctly sense what your body is craving. Why can't he get this right? Surely he doesn't think you actually want Applebee's. It's like he doesn't even know you. How have you stayed together this long? This person is flawed.
5. Dramatically declare your appetite ruined and you don't even want to eat. Just never mind. Channel your inner preschooler. Make sure body language communicates petulance.

6. Get into a medium-grade fight.

7. Have a lightbulb moment and declare the exact perfect restaurant! You saved the date! You came through! You are such a good partner! You are clutch.

8. Remember that you are starting your period tomorrow, which may account for just.a.wee.bit of your big feelings this evening. Do not share that information with your husband, because he cannot be trusted with it. If he gives you that I-knew-it look at this point, you might accidentally stab him in the eardrum with your steak knife, and that is no way to go down. Give the man a chance to live. It's date night.

HOW TO HANDLE A TWEEN WITH ATTITUDE

1. Read eight books with conflicting advice. Choose a course. (This is arbitrary.)

2. Set her down and explain the new rules in a June-and-Ward–level family meeting.

3. Be consistent for fifteen entire minutes.

4. Become increasingly irritated when tween won't act like the book described. She is nothing like "Annie" in chapter 6. Annie transforms from tyrant to model child after two strategic sentences from the Book Mom, but when *you* reply, "What I hear you saying is this makes you feel unsure and scared, which is why you are choosing anger instead of constructive words," your kid rolls her eyes and asks why you are talking so weird.

5. Lose your mind and start to boil.

6. Begin yelling things about how Annie is nice to her mother and has a lot of Jesus in her heart.
7. Pour wine. (Could also insert straw directly in bottle or box. Your call here. There is flexibility on this step.)
8. Resolve to try again tomorrow with tactics from a different book.

Programming Note: This last step could be repeated for infinity until your daughter goes to college. The parenting section at Barnes & Noble is quite large. Surely one of those books can fix adolescence.

How to Get a Good Night's Rest with Young Children

1. Hahahahaha! There is no such thing. Just put them to bed and satirically say, "Good night." You're making a joke. This is comedy. You are so funny! It is not a good night. You will see them sixteen times before sunrise. Go make yourself a second pot of coffee.

Programming Note: There is one way. Send 'em to Grandma's, and put your phone on silent.

How to Get Some Quiet Time

1. Wait until husband comes home.
2. Tell husband you have to poop. And also you have your period. This will ensure his physical and auditory distance.

3. Lock self in bathroom.
4. Pull out stash of chocolate and/or wine you have strategically and masterfully hidden behind the cleaning supplies under the sink since no one cleans except you.
5. Eat chocolate and/or drink wine, both deeply spiritual acts. Feel good about this. Feel holy.

Programming Note: Could also stash beach novel with chocolate and wine. If husband knocks after prolonged time in the bathroom, tell him you are constipated. This should buy you another twenty minutes.

How to get funny looks from your child's Sunday school teacher

1. Play "Uptown Funk" in the car on the way to church.
2. Send your three-year-old who has trouble pronouncing his n's to class while still singing the chorus. (Bonus points if he's the pastor's kid.)

How to survive your first year in Texas as a transplant

1. Speak about gun control, politics, immigration, and football with no one. (This rule has some flexibility if you live in Hippie Austin, the only blue county in a very red state. It is a hard-core boundary everywhere else.)

2. Embrace saying *y'all* immediately, and forgo all criticism of this expression. (See also: *all y'all, fixin' to, bless her, Mama and them,* and *cain't never could.*) (Also, all soft drinks are called Coke.)

3. Pledge allegiance to THE Texas grocery store: HEB. It's your new home. There is no other.

4. Wear your non-Texan football team gear only in your own home under the cover of night (see step 1).

5. Carry bug repellent with you at all times. This is non-negotiable.

6. Wear no makeup and never wash your hair in the summer. Sweat and the messy bun are your new BFFs.

7. Embrace queso as the fifth food group.

8. Drive by Jen Hatmaker's house, which you saw on HGTV, and take a selfie with it. Post this on social media and tag to Jen's page. This is not at all weird and doesn't happen every single day.

9. Drive two hours to Waco and post photos on Instagram so your friends think Chip and Joanna are your next-door neighbors.

10. Don't even think about thwarting Texas propaganda. Resistance is futile. You will end up drinking the Kool-Aid. Just give in. You cain't never help it.

How to Guarantee the Dog Will Throw Up on Your Bed

Option 1: Get a brand-new quilt, comforter, or duvet.
Option 2: Wash current one.

Programming Note: If company is also arriving the next day, this is guaranteed.

HOW TO SURVIVE A PUBLIC RESTROOM WITH YOUR PRESCHOOLER

1. Assume that they will say something untimely and brutally honest like, "Mom, it stinks in here! It stinks so bad! Mommy, did you hear me? It really stinks!"

2. When it is clear she is oblivious to your facial contortions, gently but firmly cover her mouth with your hand. Brace yourself for the muffled question, "Mommy! Why are you covering my mouth?"

3. Resign yourself to hiding in a stall until the mystery pooper exits the bathroom.

4. While in there, do not make the fatal mistake of using the facilities yourself unless you want your offspring to yell, "Mommy, you have a big vagina! Why does your tummy fold over like that? Are you going number two? Girls have three holes!"

5. Practice containing gag reflex when your little one licks the tampon repository to see "how it tastes," then lays down on the ground curled around the toilet base. Remind yourself she is building immunities.

6. Apologize to the mystery pooper as your daughter reaches under the stall and tickles her ankles. You are very, very sorry. Your kid is being terribly creepy.

7. Finally, wash every bit of exposed skin you can find in the bathroom sink, and douse her in antibacterial gel. Avoid her kisses, because that nasty mouth licked the tampon box.

Programming Note: If the child is still in a pull-up and the emergency is only number one, consider the sage advice to *Just pee in your pants.*

HOW TO HAVE A ROMANTIC EVENING AT HOME WITH YOUR HUBBY WHEN YOU HAVE LITTLE KIDS

1. Sacrifice naptime to shower and shave and dry your hair. This rare occurrence signals Sexy Time to the husband. Plus, you resemble a sasquatch down there. May need to bring scissors into the shower. We can only ask so much of our razors.
2. Work yourself to death getting all daily chores done and have kids bathed and in PJs before the hubs gets home from work. This alone is so exhausting that you almost go to bed at 6:15 p.m., but then you remember your grooming labor from earlier and don't want to waste it.
3. Order pizza for dinner so the minions will just eat and be done without spending an hour raging against vegetables. Make popcorn and water cups, and send children to the basement for a "super fun movie night."
4. Tell older children Mommy and Daddy are folding laundry and will check on them later.
5. Run to bedroom and lock door. Begin grown-up time.
6. Get paged by the eight-year-old over the ill-conceived intercom that the four-year-old needs his butt wiped. Dash to basement; clean preschooler standing with his hands around his ankles singing about potty time. This deeply contributes to your sexy mood.
7. Run back upstairs and lock door. Recommence parent snuggling.
8. Get paged again by the eight-year-old that they are out of popcorn and someone spilled their juice. Instruct eight-year-old to just "put a towel on it" and grab some chips from the pantry himself.
9. Re-recommence "Mommy and Daddy Time."

10. Eight-year-old again. The six-year-old pushed a button, and the TV isn't working. Zip back downstairs half dressed, fix TV, haul large ottoman in front of all reachable buttons, and scurry back upstairs.
11. Sexy Time, Take 4.
12. Get walked in on by three-year-old scared of "bad guys" and asking why Daddy is squishing Mommy. Soothe scared child, get a snack, put child back in the TV room, close the gate, sprint back upstairs, double-check the lock on the door, embrace husband.
13. Do not even make it past first base before all the children bound up the steps, banging on the door wondering why it is locked and screaming that the movie is over. Give up in hopeless defeat. Pile everyone on your bed to watch Mickey Mouse, and wonder how you managed to have all these kids in the first place.
14. Pretend husband might enjoy grooming ministry later that night. This will be the last conscious thought you have until your three-year-old pokes you in the eye at 6:13 a.m. asking for milk and clean clothes since he peed in your bed.

Programming Note: Motherhood is so glamorous!

How to make your house look clean while you have been watching Netflix all day, because you really, really needed to finish the series you're locked into

1. Realize it's five o'clock and husband will be home in thirty minutes.

2. Run to master bedroom and make bed. Shove miscellaneous junk in closet, bottom drawer, and on your side of the bed.
3. Take off pajamas (oops) and put on clean yoga pants, bra, and shirt. Redo bun. If hair is unrecoverable and beyond even dry shampoo, put on cute hat. Wipe yesterday's makeup from underneath your eyes.
4. Brush teeth! If face still looks sketchy, smear on lip gloss.
5. Take the laundry hamper to laundry room and empty it.
6. Take clean laundry to room husband never goes in.
7. Throw dishes in dishwasher.
8. Spray Febreze in all rooms.
9. Act like you have been cleaning all day and can't bear to mess up the kitchen. Ask to go out for dinner.

HOW TO GET YOUR KIDS TO LEAVE YOU ALONE AND GET OUT OF THE LIVING ROOM

1. Tell them to clean the playroom. They will promptly play with the toys they ignore 97 percent of the time. This doesn't matter to you. You don't care about the clean playroom. You just want some silence. You are faking them out, because you are a smart lady.
2. Approximately every thirty minutes, randomly call out, "You better be cleaning."
3. For good measure, turn on the Food Network in the living room.
4. When husband comes home and asks where the kids are, say, "Cleaning the playroom," with a knowing look on your face. Laugh like villains because you are in on this trick

together. The inmates are not running *your* asylum! Crack those long-overdue beers and finish last night's episode of *NCIS*.

HOW TO FIND A MISSING CHILD

1. Prepare to take a shower or go to the bathroom.
2. Shut door.

Programming Note: The missing child should barge in immediately, but should this method fail, silently open a candy bar or start a very important phone call. Look down: there is your kid.

HOW TO HAVE COMPANY OVER

1. Frantically clean for five hours. Get mad at everyone for being so gross. Feel very, very cranky.
2. Follow your children and husband around like a lunatic picking up everything after them, so it appears your house always looks like this, like a model home that nobody lives in. Where are the shoes and the papers and the crap? You don't have any. This is how orderly you live. Fine, they are all in the front closet.
3. Lose your mind when you find out your husband pooped in the guest bathroom just before their arrival. Spray hairspray and Windex, because your middle schooler used all the air freshener on his clothes instead of washing them.
4. Greet your guests with a smile and apologize for your house

being "so messy," even though it hasn't been this clean in six months.

5. Enjoy it, because your house will be destroyed again by tomorrow afternoon. This is your lot in life until you are a grandma.

At *family* gatherings where you suddenly feel homicidal or suicidal, remember that in half of all cases, it's a *miracle* that this annoying person even *lived*. Earth is Forgiveness School. You might as well start at the dinner table. That way, you can do this work in *comfortable* pants.[1]

–ANNE LAMOTT

CHAPTER 18

FORGIVENESS SCHOOL

A few years ago, my heart got broken. My husband's too. It centered on one primary relationship but spidered out to several others. It was easily the lowest point in our adult lives. Basically one day we were holding all the important pieces in our hands, and the next day they were all shattered: Brandon's job, several close relationships, our reputation, our security. It all erupted in a blaze of turmoil and left us reeling for one entire year, the better part of a second, and, truthfully, to the edge of a third. Some loss we predicted with perfect accuracy, but the unexpected collateral damages hurt almost worse.

We felt betrayed, misrepresented, and wounded.

And after a while, grief turned to fury and fury to contempt.

Now, years and tons of emotional and spiritual work later, I can look back and see that long after the actual injury had receded, my bitterness continued to poison. Good grief, on paper we rebuilt, rebounded, recovered in every other way. In fact, we thrived in our next season. Ancillary relationships were either restored or appropriately culled, and there were no tangible effects left to mend.

And yet, despite the outward healing—new job, new location, new mission, new partners, new season—inwardly, I was still unraveling. I continued to have furious conversations in my head, ones I'd never actually voice. I replayed the worst parts of the story, defending and countering, supplying fresh new life to my anger for years. I reveled in every disparaging bit of gossip I heard and cast God on "my side," allowing my role in the melee to shrink and the wrongs against me to inflate. I granted all my extra energy to maintaining the offense, and it turned me into a bitter cynic.

I specifically remember Brandon walking into the bathroom while I was staring in the mirror, perfecting my Face of Fury but Also Nonchalance because *I don't really care obviously* and giving a speech to my reflection. Out loud. I was practicing my righteous confrontation and massaging my finer points, making sure my body language communicated both aggression and authority while still oozing with all nine gifts of the Spirit. I don't care what Brandon said about this imaginary altercation (something about being an unstable mad hatter blah blah blah); I was totally winning that argument, and there was no way he could prove I wasn't. I was in hard-core training, like a professional athlete.

Thus the eroding effect of unforgiveness.

I approach this tender topic with caution, because I know some sins against you were heinous, good reader. Some were "unforgivable" in a court of law or in the long tale of public opinion. Perhaps your abuser went unpunished, your betrayer is unrepentant. Some wounds have visceral effects financially and structurally. Certain wounds hurt feelings, some hurt bodies, some entire families. There are degrees of harm, and not all pain is equal. Our paths to health vary, but we all have this common denominator as the foundation of healing:

Forgiveness.

Oh, it is so terrible, isn't it? Just awful. It is the one thing we don't want to give. Maybe it helps to discuss what forgiveness *is not* first. Let it be said: forgiveness is not condoning evil, not forgetting, not brushing something under the carpet, not a free pass. It does not mean minimizing the injury and, consequently, your pain. It doesn't shrink an offense down, making it smaller in memory, in impact. It doesn't shrug off loss with a "no real harm, no real foul" response. It does not mean conceding, surrendering to a different version, or yielding your right to dignity. It never communicates that this didn't happen, it didn't matter, or it didn't harm.

Furthermore, it might not mean reconciliation. Some breaches are restored and relationships mended, but some are not safe. They may never be safe. The other person may be entirely unsorry, and there is no path to harmony. Forgiving chronic abusers does not include jumping back into the fire while it is still burning; that is not grace but foolishness. Forgiveness operates in an entirely different lane than reconciliation; sometimes those roads converge and sometimes they never meet. Forgiveness is a one-man show.

One last thing: forgiveness rarely equals a one-and-done decision. Very few decide one day to forgive and never have to revisit that release. In most cases, it is a process that takes months and sometimes years of work, and just when you think you have laid an offense down, it creeps back up in memory and you have to battle it anew. Just because this work is stubborn does not mean you are failing or will never be free. Forgiveness is a long road in the same direction.

Do you ever get the impulse to hang on for dear life? Like someone should stand guard over your injury, and if no one else will, you better? Nurturing anger feels fair, a witness to injustice, like it might hold an open door for acknowledgment or forthcoming repentance or confirmation. If you forgive, where is your justice? Where is your apology? How will this ever be made right? Keeping an offender on the hook leaves room for *judgment*, which we want deferred for our own sins but rigorously applied to those inflicted on us.

But I've learned keeping someone on the hook really only keeps me on the hook. In attempting to lock up an offender, I imprison myself, captive to anger, defensiveness, and pain, replaying a story that becomes a mental loop I cannot escape from, trapping other innocent relationships and scenarios in a toxic spiral that poisons everything. I act out of woundedness instead of freedom, which makes me paranoid and suspicious, crushing everything Christlike and tender and creating a worse mess than I had in the first place. God called us to a forgiving path, not only for a mended community but also for mended human hearts.

Brennan Manning wrote, "This is the God of the gospel of grace. A God who, out of love for us, sent the only Son He ever had wrapped in our skin. He learned how to walk, stumbled and fell, cried for His milk, sweated blood in the night, was lashed with a whip and showered with spit, was fixed to a cross, and died whispering forgiveness on us all."[1] Jesus walked this sacred road first; we cannot claim His mercies without also claiming His practices. We mustn't expect a resurrected life when we skip over the cost, the commission, the cross.

Back when I was nurturing my anger, I'd spend a good half day replaying, remembering words, conversations, correspondence. I practiced comebacks and defensive maneuvers, poking holes in the other story like a State Champion debater. I'd reread e-mails and talk through it all yet again with Brandon or whoever would listen, God bless and keep anyone near me during that season. I expended a great deal of energy, getting worked up again, re-furious, re-hurt. I mourned fresh an apology that was never coming. If I was feeling it, I worked up some tears. I tidied up the narrative a bit more, removing nuance and defining motives, leaving me cleaner and the offender dirtier than we actually were. I imagined catastrophe befalling that person, which made me profoundly happy.

You know what that other person likely did that day? Ate a sandwich, answered some e-mails, had a meeting, returned some pants to the mall. I was the only one paying the piper, spending energy and mental space not on healing but on imagined vindication. What a waste! That person was not on the hook in the slightest, but I sure was, day after day, month after month, disastrously, year after year. I deferred my own peace, and the only loss was mine.

The work of forgiveness is so challenging—the actual work of it. The naming, grieving, empathizing, releasing. It's like a death. A death of what we wanted, what we expected, what we'd hoped for, what we deserved and didn't receive. Burying those expectations, because they are indeed dead, is truly cause for grief. Expect to feel profound loss as you put them six feet under. Into the casket also goes control, exoneration, maybe even resolution. Those don't belong to you. We don't get to control other people or outcomes. I am as devastated about this as you.

How to begin? Oh heavenly mercies. There isn't a template for this work, but I can tell you my early steps to forgiveness. God was super clear: *Pray for this person every day*, which was the meanest thing He ever said to me. I was furious. I think I even said something petulant to God like, "The hell I will!" and He was all, "Do it, Potty Mouth." So my prayers started rather, well, shallow: *Please don't let this person get hit by a car today. Amen.* That was as far as I could go. The anger around my heart was still stretched tight. I was obedient to the letter of the law only.

But as that practice went on, something started to happen. God loosened that old anger bit by bit, and the prayers gave way to deeper, more meaningful requests. Mind you, the increments were small and took more time than I wanted to give, but I started thinking of that person as the kid they once were, whose story I knew included loss and abandonment. God began showing me triggers I had ignited carelessly, tapping into lifelong wounds that set off a disproportional reaction. Prayer awakened enough humility to own my contribution to the free fall, a difficult admission. And would you believe after staying the course long enough, I developed a tenderness toward the person who hurt us, and it was sincere. Prayer didn't heal the relationship, but it healed me.

God is still in the miracle business, and sometimes those miracles are in us.

While forgiveness might feel like abandoning justice, it actually sets us free. It liberates us from the crushing responsibility to oversee the resolution, which may or may not ever come. It removes any authority another person holds over our wholeness; it steals its power. Surprisingly, it can even bring us to the point where we wish our offender well, where we desire his or her peace too. It gently takes our minds and hearts and attention and brings them back to the present, to be with the ones who are here. Forgiveness gives us back our life and gives us back to our life. It is holy and hard work that says to God: *Here is this sad thing. It is all Yours to fix or mend or redeem or simply bear witness. I am prying my hands off and freeing them up for other work.*

We bury what we wanted and accept what we have.

But then, new life. Rising up from the grave, like tender little shoots. So small at first. So fragile. But forgiveness clears the way for new growth, even if the other person is completely unrepentant. We can still live. We can still be vibrant. We grow and develop and find beauty again, shoots of hope pushing up through the rubble. And soon enough, when we nurture grace and release instead of anger and resentment, a bloom, an unfolding of life again.

Two quick words: If the person who hurt you has a history of mainly healthy behavior, if they've been mostly safe, by all means, press not only into forgiveness but reconciliation. A broken relationship mended by forgiveness can be even stronger than it was before. Henri Nouwen wrote: "Forgiveness is the name of love practiced among people who love poorly. The hard truth is that all people love poorly. We need to forgive and be forgiven every day, every hour increasingly. That is the great work of love among the fellowship of the weak that is the human family."[2] Confrontations, difficult conversations, these are hard, I know. But better to prioritize a restored relationship than let it go down without a fight simply because we are conflict averse. Earth is indeed Forgiveness School.

Second, forgiveness comes easier to people who regularly ask forgiveness themselves. It is mature Christian practice to own our offenses and remain humble enough to apologize when we've wounded, intentionally or not. This posture makes a tender people, a safer family with softer edges. All of us love poorly at some point, and infusing our community with ownership and repentance is contagious. Say you're sorry. Ask forgiveness. This leads not only to stronger relationships but to better humans, and this world needs better humans.

It is worth the work. Beth Moore wrote on Twitter: "God is raising you mighty and mighty doesn't come pretty. Pay the price." The cost of forgiveness is high but the payoff is higher: health, peace, wholeheartedness, grace. It goes on: resilience, maturity, compassion, depth. God raises us back up mighty in love, through the pain, through the mess, stronger than before. Forgiveness does not erase your past—a healed memory is not a deleted memory—but it does enlarge your future, increase your love, and set you free.

It's worth it.

Wine is constant *proof* that God loves us and loves to see us *happy*.[1]

–BENJAMIN FRANKLIN

CHAPTER 19

POTATO AND KNIFE

My body completely behaved in my twenties. It delivered three babies like a boss, snapped back into shape no matter what the mouth fed the stomach, and it crossed the Thirty Threshold in a minuscule size six. What a mannerly body! What a champion! What a trooper! What an underappreciated star with a clear shelf life!

These days, the first number on the scale is the same but the second is the difference between a toddler and an independent reader, God bless us each and every one. My body's history communicates an obvious possibility, a size I actually was even after being pregnant twenty-seven out of fifty-six months, but it can't figure out how to get back there, or really even near there. After careful analysis, I think I've narrowed the problem down:

Food. And drinks.

All of them.

I love basically all the food and all the drinks.

I worship everything that no one eats anymore: dairy, gluten, carbs, wheat, sugar, red wine. These are my best friends. I want to marry gluten, and the rest of these beauties can be my brides-maids. Chips and salsa can walk me down the aisle. My favorite food is a toasted sandwich with mayo (Duke's, of course) and fresh tomato slices and melted Swiss and ham and bread-and-butter pickles. I cannot live without pizza, nor would I want to. Deep red wine and bruschetta and salty aged Gouda is my Camelot. A juicy burger on a soft homemade bun with blue cheese and cara-melized onions alongside crispy Parmesan fries is my life force.

Sure, I could just not eat those, but I want to is the thing. I love them. Spicy flavors and melted ooziness and crunchy browned things and rich, fragrant sauces make me supremely, delightfully, viscerally happy. I want to cook them, share them, eat them, talk about them, write about them, gush over them, read about them, go bananas over them. I have no qualms discussing a brilliant dinner I am eating the whole time I am eating it. This is how I weed out friend candidates—if they cannot continue to rhapso-dize after the first course, if they are unwilling to *share bites*, like a terrorist, we have no future.

Somehow for me, cooking ends up being greater than the sum of its parts. Alone, prepping veggies sounds tedious, scour-ing recipes takes too much planning, cooking for an hour after a workday seems like punishment. But altogether, the alchemy of the smells and sounds, the music playing and glass of peppery Cabernet nearby, the physical rhythm of chopping, stirring, and searing after a day of thinking, sitting, and typing turns into my favorite section of the day, when work fades and the family starts to gather near the kitchen because sizzling garlic and onion is an irresistible temptress. Cooking dinner is a sacred gateway from work to rest, from seven separate lives to one shared table.

And for the record before we go on, dinner is absolutely my day's last hurrah. My mom is still chewing her last bite as she starts cleaning the kitchen. I think she has gone to bed with a dirty kitchen never. I, on the other hand, have no problem leaving mine a war zone. As long as the food is put up (I am a leftover evangelist), I can plop right down on the couch for my end-of-the-day Netflix prize and leave the mess until dawn. It's my last gasp, the cooking. With the fed bellies and happy eaters and kids retiring to homework, I discover I am D.O.N.E. *Thank you, Austin! That's my show! You've been amazing!* Consequently, my tank drops from half full to terrifyingly empty in five minutes, making the Bedtime Hour treacherous for all parties involved.

Related: I feel like a Catholic at confession, and I'm not sure how to say this without alienating my tribe and showing my cards, but as it turns out, I am a Morning Mom. I actually feel embarrassed about this. Like my brand of sarcasm and melodrama requires crankiness in the a.m. It would be such good material. But nope. No, ma'ams. I am full of hope and promise in the morning. *Good morning, lovies! Good morning, good morning, good mooooorning, it's time to rise and shine!* I am all cheek kisses and back rubs and gentle words and sunshine at dawn's early light.

Brandon wakes up the kids like a drill sergeant at boot camp. Morning requires Discipline and No Whining and his little soldiers better hup to. He throws their lights on and refuses to coddle sleepy, warm teens and preteens. He is not having it. But I am having all of it. Your honor, I submit as evidence the fact that I still wake up all my children, though one of them is old enough to vote. Breakfast tacos, delicious smoothies, waffles and bacon, baked oatmeal; I cook breakfast every morning like an annoying Cream of Wheat ad. Here is some fresh salsa for your migas; here are sliced bananas for your pancakes. It is obnoxious. Does it help you still like me knowing that I have none of this energy past dinner and that I "pray with Remy" while she is in her bed and I am yelling a prayer to Christ our Lord from the living room?

For me, there is something deeply satisfying in feeding my

people well. It helps that they mostly love yummy food and appreciate the work, but even then, it feels good, like I prioritized something important, something nourishing and healthy. Maybe it's because I am not inherently nurturing; I lean no-nonsense. I don't really coddle or fuss or hover or overprotect. I don't like to play board games. I'm not sweet. I was always rubbish at Legos ("Mommy, all you build are towers"). I'm of the Buck Up, Buttercup crowd. So cooking real food with my hands that tastes good is my way of taking actual, physical care of my people. It is me saying: *I love you, I care about you, I care for you.* It is my offering.

We live in a small town adjacent to Austin, right off old-fashioned Main Street. It is as quaint and charming as you think, a movie set in real life. We walk to the little restaurants and coffee shop and library all the time, the train an ever-present soundtrack. At Cleveland's, a restaurant in a 130-year-old building with original wide plank floors and a tin ceiling, I was swooning over their French fries, rustic and flavorful and irregular, when the waiter, not just a server but a foodie, said: "Just potato and knife. It's enough."

We've lost a little something in today's microwave world, haven't we? The best path to the perfect French fry has always been running a sharp knife through actual potatoes, dropping them in bubbling oil or baking in a searing oven, then sprinkling crunchy salt all over them while they are still hot. But somewhere along the way, *potato and knife* became processed, frozen fries—uniform, coated, tasteless, covered in ice shards. Food turned complicated and industrialized. It was once pretty basic: garden, tree, animal, plants. Now it is fat-free, high fructose corn syrup, flavor coated, dyed. It is prepackaged, quick and easy, freezer to table, no fuss.

And believe me, I understand the appeal of those words. If anything in my day can be quick and easy, I am here for it, and

I'll run through the Taco Bell drive-thru in a hot minute on days our family is the center attraction at the Freak Show Circus. However, we hand off much more than labor to the food industry, not the least of which is nutrition, but perhaps the greater loss is the beautiful farm-to-table system God devised down here. There is something noble about real food, the exchange between farmer and eater, the simple transformation of raw ingredients into breakfast, into dinner. There is also honor in the work, the cooking. It is old-fashioned, an homage to our mothers and grandmothers and all mothers and grandmothers in the history of time.

Here is the right place to affirm that cooking doesn't have to be fancy or complicated or take two hours a night. The industrialized food industry nestled those lies deep within the ethos of their marketing strategy: *cooking real food will be too hard for your busy life and skill set . . . we got this for you.* But let me assure you that simple, homemade food does not require a culinary degree or half your evening. It is cheaper than processed, prepackaged stuff, and anyone can dice an onion, roast sweet potatoes, grill lamb burgers.

I've also learned that kids (and husbands, oh my gosh) will eventually start eating what you cook. If all we ever serve is frozen nuggets and canned corn, obviously they will buck curried fried rice. But if you start incorporating new flavors and new ingredients and new combinations bit by bit, if you slowly introduce sesame green beans or chopped salad or fish tacos and start seasoning your food with zingy flavors, you can indeed broaden your family's palate. In my opinion, it is worth the aggravation this food odyssey will initially deliver by way of complaining, fussing, overreacting, and full-on lamenting (these poor people having to eat red peppers; THE HUMANITY).

Finally, before I give you a recipe so you, too, can outpace your twentysomething body (I am here for you), let me say this: I cook dinner around three days a week. This feels like a smashing victory. On the other days, we eat leftovers, takeout, random food, or FFY (Fend For Yourself). This bothers me zero percent. I have not batted 1,000 for any single category in the whole of my life. I love food, I love cooking, I love the entire thing, and I still manage less than half a week. So everyone be cool. Gather up all your chill and do the best you can, even if that means one day of homemade and six days of Count Chocula. If these children don't like it, they can grow up and move out one day and make their own dinners, and may God bless them with kids who only eat processed cheese slices on white bread.

This is a great homemade recipe for your repertoire. I'm going to give you a winner, so your nonadventurous eaters won't gripe, but you can still push the envelope just a smidge.

FRIED CHICKEN SLIDERS WITH HONEY DIJONNAISE

This is mostly homemade, partly not, but the one processed ingredient involves Hawaiian Rolls, and if we can't make an exception for those, all of life is meaningless. You have almost all these ingredients already, so a one-bag trip to the store will have you in business.

Honey Dijonnaise Sauce
1 cup mayo
2 tablespoons Dijon mustard
2 tablespoons honey
Pinch of salt

Fried Chicken:
Peanut oil (about an inch in your skillet)
2 cups milk

1 tablespoon white wine vinegar
1 egg
1 teaspoon salt
1 teaspoon pepper
1 teaspoon cayenne
2 cups all-purpose flour
1 cup panko bread crumbs
1 tablespoon each: salt, garlic powder, paprika
6 thin-cut chicken breasts, cut in half for 12 sliders (Or
    as many as you want to make. I literally make 20.)

Sliders:

1 package Hawaiian Slider Rolls, sliced in half lengthwise
1 (8-ounce) package Swiss cheese slices (or
    provolone, Colby-Jack, Cheddar, whatever)
1 pound bacon, cooked and cut in half
Lettuce
Sliced tomatoes

Make your Honey Dijonnaise: mix all the ingredients together in a small bowl. (There, you're done). Stick it in the fridge.

Now fry your chicken: pour the oil into a large flat-bottomed skillet, and start heating on medium-high heat. (Your oil has to be super hot, or you get soggy, oil-drowned fried chicken, and your family will cry all the tears in North America.)

In a shallow baking dish, combine the milk, vinegar, and egg, and mix together. This basically becomes homemade buttermilk, because who buys actual buttermilk? I throw in some seasonings here, because a bit of salt and cayenne and black pepper ain't never hurt nothin'. In a second shallow baking dish, mix the flour, panko, and seasonings.

Salt and pepper both sides of your chicken breast halves. With one hand, dip a breast into the milk mixture. Move it to the flour mixture, and toss with the other hand. (I am not trying to be difficult, good reader. Just keeping your fingers from becoming breaded.) Shake off the excess flour and place carefully into the hot oil. Fry four to five minutes on each side until Brown and Beautiful. Repeat with the rest of the chicken, but don't crowd your pan. You will probably fry in two batches. Keep your first batch in a 200-degree oven on a pan lined with paper towels.

Build your Hawaiian sliders: bread, Honey Dijonnaise, fried chicken, cheese, bacon, lettuce, tomato, Honey Dijonnaise, bread.

Listen to what I'm saying to you: This is my family's tip-top most requested meal. I am not even kidding. It's just a fried chicken sandwich for the love of Truett Cathy, but the attention to flavor on each layer, plus the dreamy sweet slider rolls, inspired this dinner conversation the last time I made these:

Caleb: Raise your hand if you think these are better than Chick-fil-A.

[All hands up.]

I rest my case.

There is nothing
else on this
earth more to
be *prized* than
true *friendship.*[1]

–THOMAS AQUINAS

CHAPTER 20

FANGIRL

've spoken often about our Supper Club, now in our fifth year of feeding one another once a month, devoted in between. There are four couples: two pastors, four authors, three business owners, three native Texans, one hipster who used to be a cowboy, one Jersey girl who used to be Goth, and sixteen kids between us. We rotate houses, the host cooks and cleans, and we never make it home before 1:00 a.m., which means SC is really two days: one for feasting and one for recovery.

In addition to all the work, the host comes up with a table discussion topic. Sometimes it is funny like, *What was your most kickass moment as a kid, when you thought you were nailing life?* (This resulted in me singing "Blue Jeans" for my compatriots, the award-winning song Christy Doucet and I sang in the sixth-grade talent show, which won first place. Stop asking me about it, you guys! You're embarrassing me!) Topics are witty, silly, or incredibly poignant and precious. I cried into my charred shrimp and jalapeño Cheddar grits just two weeks ago at Aaron and Jamie's, so dear was the conversation. Four years ago or so, one of the questions was this:

Would you rather be rich or famous?

The answers were absolutely hilarious, and along with half of SC, I said: "Famous." I know. Gross. In my defense, my reasoning was that our life was happy as is, and money wasn't that motivating, so I defaulted to fame, which seemed harmless, intangible, almost like a fake paradigm with no real effect. I guess I pick famous! Tra la la.

Girls, *forget that noise.* I've since had a small taste of that, and it is the oddest, most bizarre alternate universe ever. Being low-grade Christian famous is straight-up crazy. I only occupy a very minor corner of this zip code, enough to know what I'm talking about but not enough to make me a weirdo. I am regularly confused by my life. I do things I never planned on a hot day in my imagination: write books people read, speak on stages, talk on the radio, show up on TV sometimes. Are you kidding me with this? I wanted to be Janet Jackson or, if not that, a librarian. I taught fourth grade and married a youth pastor. This was not my life plan.

I wrote my first book in 2004. It was published in 2006 with two others I fast-tracked. I wrote three more in three years, and exactly no one read any of them or knew anything about me for the next five years. I basically worked for free, and I'm pretty sure I made negative money. I spoke at every sort of retreat, once in a living room with five women, one of whom slept through my entire "talk." At one small church, I was introduced as "Jen Hatfield," and no one corrected her because they had zero idea what my name was either. In fact, until a few years ago, when you googled my name, the same question popped up every time: *Did you mean Jean Hatmaker?*

I cannot quit laughing about Jean. I miss that girl.

Trust me: don't waste your time overvaluing Christian famous people. It is so easy to cast public figures as prototypes of discipleship or pristine examples of faithfulness, but all that admiration is totally misplaced. I mean this sincerely: only Jesus is worth your full devotion. He alone will never let you down and will always lead you correctly. The rest of us? Oh my word. We will fail you, disappoint you, and even shock you, because we are the exact same brand of human as anyone else. I am short-tempered, lazy, self-preserving, and indulgent. I do not share all your theology and interpretations, and if you look to me as your spiritual plumb line, you will be gravely disappointed, if not now, someday. Believe me. You will want to kick kittens. Sometimes my mess outpaces my moxie, and no one has the good sense to deactivate my social media accounts so I will not become an actual threat to the kingdom of God.

Idolizing human beings just isn't the way Jesus built His community to thrive. He decentralized, empowering ordinary people to be carriers of the good news. He commissioned the kingdom to mamas and daddies and fishermen and widows and fresh new believers and former terrorists. Jesus had nothing but harsh words for the Fancy Leader paradigm of His day, and for good reason: being overly admired spiritually is the death knell of integrity. It creates such a mess! To borrow Jesus's words, it protects hypocrisy, creating "cup and dish leaders" that are incredibly shiny and clean on the outside, but inside they are full of greed and self-indulgence. And that leader will not lead you well, because you will become a commodity, a means to an end, a caricature. Jesus is the sole hero, the only leader truly worth His salt.

I have a way better idea.

After my last book release, I invited my entire volunteer launch team to my house for a big party, so almost three hundred women came from virtually every state. We'd been deep diving into real life together for half a year (and still to this very day more than two years later), so coming together was less about Going to Jen's House and more about finally meeting treasured friends face-to-face. After the party, one of our girls, Corie, came up with the best solution to celebrity culture, which we'd worked terribly hard to dismantle in our little community:

Fangirl Jesus, and fangirl your friends.

Yes. Truly, I want you to freak out over Jesus. Now *that* thrills me. Save your best devotion for Him, because Jesus is so worthy of stars in our eyes, butterflies in our stomachs, heart palpitations in our chests. He really is, man. What is not to love about a guy who pulled children onto His lap and saved a failing party and touched the untouchables and told off the religious elite? I have always said that if you don't love Jesus, you just don't know Him. He is the full and complete jam, and we would all be fighting to sit by Him at dinner if He was here now (and you know He would sit by the most wretched, broken-down person there and give everyone else FOMO). I cannot wait to meet Jesus in heaven. He is my favorite.

Then fangirl the flesh and blood people around you, the ones you live by, live with, live for. Go gaga over your own people; *that* is well-placed loyalty. Overvalue *them*, over-love *them*, over-encourage *them*. Rather than overloading the top-heavy accounts, we should put far more love deposits in other columns, diversify the portfolio, spread out the investment, bank locally.

One of my girlfriends created a text rule, which basically means anytime she has a lovely thought about someone or is reminded of them in any way or notices something delightful about a person, she immediately sends them a quick text saying so. She just voice-texts it, so it is always full of weird misspellings and nonsense words (*"You are such a wonderful chair leader* [cheerleader] *for women! You practical need tampons* [pompoms]*!"*), but she sends the love before the thought leaves her mind, which increases the chance of delivery by around 100 percent. This is not taxing or hard or time-consuming, but she fangirls people better than anyone. We live for her texts.

Fangirl the people who never get fangirled. You know the ones: the underdog, the quiet hero, the little guy. They are shy or behind the scenes or difficult or loners. It's boring when the same old obvious people get all the enthusiasm; the spotlight naturally gravitates toward certain folks in our culture, those who fit the template. But the earth is jam-packed with amazing, extraordinary people who color outside the narrow lines society deems noteworthy, and they deserve applause too.

Remy's elementary school has grade-level awards ceremonies every nine weeks where they celebrate all kinds of achievements: academic, social, physical, relational. The end of the year includes overall, yearlong awards voted on by the kids. Last year, building suspense with dramatic pauses, our principal called up the Buda Elementary Employee of the Year: Head Custodian Josie Garza. She *ran* up to the stage, shell-shocked with both hands covering her face. The entire auditorium lost their minds, and I choked down sobs until I nearly passed out. Quiet, gentle, accomplishing her hard workday in and day out with generosity and cheerfulness—what a joy to fangirl Ms. Garza! Three cheers for all the Ms. Garzas! May we find them, love them, and celebrate them.

I realize some of you are lonely, and no one is texting *you* love notes when they catch *you* being awesome. I'll give the same advice I give my kids when they are struggling socially: If you want to make good friends, be a good friend. Send kindness out in big, generous waves, send it near and far, send it through texts and e-mails and calls and words and hugs, send it by showing up, send it by proximity, send it in casseroles, send it with a well-timed "me too," send it with abandon. Put out exactly what you hope to draw in, and expect it back in kind and in equal measure.

I am so convinced we reap what we sow here; sow seeds of affirmation and goodness and grace into others, and you will reap the devotion of well-loved friends. You will. You cannot love others genuinely and generously and have it return void for long. Convinced my dance card was full with no room for new relationships, I have literally had some now dear friends *wear me the freak down* with kindness (and sarcasm because that is my primary love language), like a rushing river of love eventually smoothing out this jagged, call-screening rock until I eventually said, "FINE. I love you. My gosh, you made me."

Inversely, sow seeds of silence or uninvolvement or high-maintenance entitlement, and you will likely reap an empty inbox. I mean this tenderly, sisters. Psalms tells us that "deep calls to deep," and similarly, grace calls to grace, joy calls to joy, laughter calls to laughter, sincerity calls to sincerity. Unfortunately in the same way, drama calls to drama, dysfunction calls to dysfunction, bitterness calls to bitterness, cynicism calls to cynicism. We get back what we put out. We have so much say-so in our own relational experience. Be the friend you'd love to have, call to the deep, and you will attract the treasured kind of friends like sunlight, like a lightning rod, like honey.

Fangirl your friends.

This would be so good for all of us. No need to fangirl this yahoo. Let's free one another up to occupy appropriate roles for one another as encouragers and cheerleaders, fellow learners and dreamers, like friends, like allies, like sisters. That feels safe and right and good to me. I'm all here for that, for you, for us. Be good to each other. Let's heal the world together. We each have a note to play, and I'm glad to play mine, grateful to be a tiny part in a big, beautiful, wonderful, sisterhood song.

From birth to age 18 a girl
needs good *parents*.
From 18 to 35 she needs
good *looks*. From 35
to 55 she needs a good
personality. From 55
on, she needs *cash*.[1]

–SOPHIE TUCKER

ﾟℓℓℴ

CHAPTER 21

WE WERE SORT
OF MEDIUM

Dear Parents,
   Mom, today is your sixty-fifth birthday, which means
you and Dad are both officially able to retire as well as receive the
senior discount at Luby's. Congratulations. You cannot beat the
Luann Platter for $5.99. Your son and oldest grandson would be
happy to take you there to celebrate, because, as you know, they
are Luby's evangelists. Grandma King raised us right; we love a
cafeteria.

   Anyway, I thought I'd write you and Dad some thoughts on
Growing Up King. The sibs and I have discussed and have nearly
identical assessments. The only departure is their extra gratitude
for getting bailed out of jail. As the sole dependent who hasn't
seen the inside of a cell, I confess I have lied to you about a bunch
of other stuff, so let's just call it even and leave you to bask in the
glow of no longer raising us. Teenagers are delightful! (We cannot
believe you were teetotalers back then.)

One of the lamest things about raising kids is how they don't fully appreciate you until they are grown. What a chore to suffer the self-righteousness, exasperated sighs, and sassy mouths, and you endured all that and then some. I mean, we were some oppressed children (roll eyes here). Would it have killed you to buy one pair of Guess jeans and subscribe to MTV? Nobody knew the trouble we saw.

But then we grew up and discovered we'd had an amazing childhood. My first clue came in college when tons of my friends had broken families and worked three jobs to put themselves through school. It never even occurred to me to worry about funding my degree, much less detaching from toxic parents. As it turned out, we'd been cradled in security since the day we were born. Oh sure, we didn't have much money, but I had no idea. Our life never felt scarce or fragile. *Now* I know you scrimped and worried, but we never felt that then. You gave us real security, the kind that settles down in your bones and insulates you from fear. (To this day, I cannot muster up much fear. I am overconfident in this world and its people, which you can either take the blame or credit for.)

We have reams to be thankful for. I could fill the rest of this book with it. But since this is just a letter, not a comprehensive family history, I thought I'd mention three specific gifts you gave us:

First, thank you for raising us in a fun and funny home. Our house was filled to the rafters with laughter and absurdity. We were not overly earnest or intense, and we learned that a healthy life meant taking a handful of things incredibly seriously and most other things less seriously. You never majored on minors, and it liberated us from a sense of failure. Some of my friends were criticized within an inch of their lives growing up, and they still struggle deeply with self-assurance, contentment, joy. There is a place for a "no big deal" outlook, for the ability to laugh instead of cringe, to find humor instead of offense. We were not constantly avoiding critique, so we were free to just be normal kids with laid-back parents who quoted funny movies. To say nothing of piling into one bed with Dad every night while he told demented bed-time stories like "The Electrocution and Dismemberment of the Big Bad Wolf" and that time he and Uncle Tom shot Grandma's cats because they slept on their freshly waxed cars. Sweet dreams, kids.

It worked out. Plus, we are hilarious now. Remember that girlfriend Drew had a few years ago who never laughed at our jokes and didn't respond to our Gold Material? *Goodbye and god-speed, ma'am.* You (mainly Dad) groomed sweeping, dramatic storytellers; we can take one small experience and turn it into a stand-up routine. It is an obnoxious, self-congratulatory skill set, but here we are. It's so fun to be together as grown-ups, because someone will always be on. If not us, our spouses, because humor was obviously a marriage prerequisite. Like the time Zac told us about his high school garage band Burning Animosity: "We didn't sing or play instruments, but we were going to learn. What mattered was that we had a band name. Then life happened. Someone fell in love. Someone got grounded. Stuff went down. Story as old as time." No one makes us laugh like ZZ.

Fun and funny is underrated. It's interesting—laughter has a way of drowning out lesser memories; it pulls through as the lead story. We certainly had dark seasons and sorrows and mis-steps, like that time you slapped me across the face for just *telling my truth, Mom,* but those didn't leave the most lasting impression. They didn't become the headline. They were subplots beneath the primary storyline of love and security.

This gives me hope as I am still neck deep in family minutia here; time hasn't minimized the failures or monotony or the daily crapshoot of supervising five kids. It's all still a bit too precious, and I regularly worry the latest misfire will be the thing they'll remember most. So acknowledging the staying power of *general tone* over *particulars* is such a comfort; hopefully they'll remember the laughter more than that time I threw all their dirty laundry in the backyard.

Second, thanks for being super into us. We grew up with fans. I'd be remiss not to single you out here, Dad, because your particular brand of enthusiasm is, as we all know, legendary. All four of us sincerely believed we were special children, that the universe blessed us with talent and charm, intelligence and wit. We bought all your hype. You believed in us irrationally, which made us accidentally confident. We were solidly in our twenties before discovering we were just sort of medium, but by that point, it was too late; we missed the window of insecurity and entered adulthood like, *Here we are!* (And the world was like, *So?* Which did not deter us in the slightest.)

Heaven have mercy on the authorities that didn't recognize our specialness or, dare I recall, oppressed us: teachers, coaches, principals, neighbors, bosses, academic deans, other parents, arresting officers—they faced many a losing battle, those poor souls. And sure, Dad, you mainly led this brigade, but Mom occasionally went Red Rage, too, like that time my media teacher gave me the only C in the class, *a class with no real grades*, because he didn't like me. (It is no wonder he retired the next year.) To this day, Dad, you offer to censure social media haters with *a swift word*, but since I am a forty-two-year-old grown adult person, having my dad defend me on Facebook is probably unnecessary.

Another childhood staple that permanently affected my trajectory was your liberal and generous commitment to your friends. Your friends (and consequently their kids) were such a constant presence in our life, we grew up assuming genuine community was a given. We spent as much time at your friends' houses as our own, and I can hardly remember a vacation or trip or Sunday night barbecue without another family or two with us. We watched you and your friends laugh and cry and group parent us together, and it set a vitally important bar for my life: healthy adult friends are a priority and life is better alongside them.

I never knew otherwise, so I pursued wholehearted, wholly devoted friendships as an adult. My friends are so deeply embedded in our life that I honestly cannot picture my story without them. I grew up learning transparency and vulnerability, commitment and solidarity. I never had to read a book on "developing natural community," because childhood was my classroom and you were my teachers. I learned the secret sauce by experience: time together and lots of it, laughter, truth telling, grace, authenticity, God. It became as natural as the air I breathe: friends matter.

In a very rare moment of transparency, another pastor's wife once confided that despite her easy breezy lively persona, she actually had no real friends, because the vulnerability was too risky. She "gave women just enough to feel connected to her" but nothing real. She and her husband were locked away on their own island, friendly with many but committed to none, and not one person actually knew her. It was maybe the saddest thing I'd ever heard. Thank you for teaching me to love and be loved by friends fully, entirely, recklessly, because my life is immensely richer for it.

I am in what one of my favorite writers, Kelly Corrigan, calls "The Middle Place" (which you obviously know because I made us all read her book since her father, Greenie, is Dad's personality twin). That wonderful sweet spot as an active mom but still very much someone's daughter. If I could, I would freeze time to preserve these treasured years with all my kids at home while having vibrant, healthy parents. It is so comforting that even while spinning all the plates of career, ministry, marriage, and parenthood, at your house I am still just your oldest kid who may or may not help with the dishes. I still crave your approval and want to make you proud. I still want you to tell me what to do sometimes. My car still heads straight to your house in moments of crisis. When we suffered a bit of collapse last year, I told Brandon at the onset: "I just need to call my mom."

As you know, we are starting to launch our kids out into the world, and my greatest hope is to begin adult relationships with them that look something like ours. On days when grief overtakes me and I feel profound loss at their departure, I remember that just last Sunday, twenty-four years after I moved to college, I ate pot roast at your house after church and took a nap on your couch. This is not an ending but a new beginning. If we have been to our kids anything at all like the parents you were to us, I can look forward to grown sons and daughters sauntering back through my door constantly, still very much into their parents and perfectly happy to eat my food and nap in my bed, maybe all living within forty-five minutes of each other.

The best dividend of a happy childhood is healthy adult relationships later. We didn't need to run from you or overcome you or heal from you. We never had to fix what you broke in us or untangle from what you said to us. You didn't saddle us with your baggage or set an impossible course in front of us. I don't have any daddy issues except trying to keep you from verbally assaulting trolls on Facebook. As evidenced by our concentrated geography, we don't want to put a thousand miles between us now or screen your calls (except when Dad is talking about hay at the ranch; I can only devote around four minutes to alfalfa). Healthy parents and a healthy childhood was a real and rare gift, and I didn't even know to be grateful until it was over.

But I am. We all are. We are so very thankful for parents who loved us well. It still brings such security to be your daughter, and I am halfway through my life. I have submitted my proposal to God for the end of your earthly lives, and it involves you dying peacefully in your sleep at the exact same time, holding hands, in forty years. I figured Dad could live to be 109 easily because he still runs four miles a day, and Mom could reach 105 because she cooked with so much oat bran from 1988 to 1991.

In the meantime, we kids will keep having babies and launching them into the world for a while, and we will still bring them all over to your house to eat baked goods and climb your trees and shoot pool while we drink wine on your porch. The middle place still has a lot of life left, so we'll store up these years like a treasure, remembering them one day just as fondly as the first phase of our family when we were dirty kids drinking water out of the backyard hose. Of course, in a hundred years, no one will remember any of us and our story will be lost in obscurity, but for us, for all these years when we were kids and then grown-ups, when you were young parents and then grandparents, this is the only story that ever mattered, and it was such a marvelous one. The best story I ever imagined.

How To
(Part Four)

How to get a toddler dressed in three easy steps

1. Pick out perfectly matched outfit the night before. Secure toddler approval before bed.
2. Show toddler outfit in the morning. Recognize a violent, abrupt change of heart.
3. Listen to thirty minutes of high-pitched wailing.
4. Try to make sense of what has happened to your life. How is this what you are doing with your Monday morning?
5. Ask toddler to pick out clothes for self with some guidance, of course.
6. Suggest a shirt to match the pants.
7. Give up and let toddler leave house wearing slippers, sparkly tutu, hair in five pigtails with multiple clips, pajama shirt, and snow pants. You can't care about everything.

How to perpetuate well-intentioned lies to your children

Phase 1: When your oldest child loses his first tooth, create a fanciful story of a beautiful tooth fairy who magically retrieves the treasured tooth from the adorable satin tooth bag under his pillow, leaving a shiny silver dollar and a trail of sparkly fairy dust from his bed to the window sill. Take seven pictures. Document in that year's album. Put on Instagram.

Phase 2: Fast-forward to the second or third child and about twenty teeth later. The satin bag is long gone. You've depleted your supply of silver dollars. You are running a crap operation now. Panic as your child greets you in the morning with sad, forlorn eyes to report that the tooth fairy didn't come (again). Feign shock at this travesty, grab a couple of dirty dollars from your wallet, and race to their room loudly insisting she must have missed it. Shove the crumpled cash under the pillow. Throw the tooth fairy under the bus to child: "She *really* needs to be more careful when she leaves her bounty. She is getting sloppy. I think she might be hitting the sauce."

Phase 3: Fourth child? No shock. You've run out of freak-outs for teeth. The freak-out drawer is empty. You casually tell your kid: "The tooth fairy left your money in my purse because you didn't pick up your toys last night and she was afraid of getting hurt stepping over them. How much? It's like $1.67 in change. Just look in the bottom of my wallet."

How to grow an insanely long chin or neck hair when you're thirty-seven

1. Blink. That should do it.

Programming Note: Attend an important outing or event in broad daylight. This should ensure your medical marvel will be not only record-breaking but easily visible to all onlookers while remaining obscured in your bathroom mirror.

HOW TO TALK TO YOUR TEENAGER

1. Slowly enter the beast's cave, throwing darting glances side to side as you scan the room for living or dead things. The smell suggests a corpse. You hope for just an old glass of milk. It's hard to know.
2. Assess teenager on bed or at computer. If thumbs and fingers are moving, texting or typing is happening. Wait for the teenage invitation: "What?!" Ah, he sees you.
3. Initiate conversation, which is mostly just you asking questions and deciphering which *yes, no, I guess*, and grunt go with each question. Good talk.
4. Casually ask teenager if he knows what aforementioned smell is and then retreat slowly as he death-stares you out the door. The smell does not affect him. He cohabitates with the smell. He defends the smell. The smell is only your problem.
5. Remind yourself he *does* love you and this is just a phase because everything is weird in his head right now, and rest assured you have the passcode to his phone (that you pay for) should you become concerned and need to read his texts later while eating popcorn.
6. Spray Febreze liberally on everything after he goes to sleep, including his actual body.

How to meet an impending deadline

1. Worry, overthink, and over-emote about the task. Make yourself a nuisance to all listening parties. Get on at least seven people's last nerve lamenting your deadline.
2. Get very serious about making a plan. Set up your workspace. Light a candle. Pray to Jesus and also to God. Set mug of steaming coffee next to your laptop. Adjust the lighting. Play gentle and unintrusive Pandora station on level two. Take deep cleansing breaths. Meditate for three to five minutes.
3. Check Facebook.
4. Check Instagram.
5. Check Twitter.
6. Open inbox. Delete junk mail. Despair at the rest. Close.
7. Open the impending task, file, program, or project. Look at it with your eyes. Think a couple of thoughts about it with your mind. Put your fingers on your keyboard. Await inspiration.
8. Organize desk. This is urgent all of a sudden. Throw away six pounds of papers. Find an old photo album. Reminisce for seventeen minutes. Take a snapshot of your high school prom and post to IG. #TBT
9. Get a snack.
10. Back to the project. Type two sentences. Abandon hope. The magic is gone. You don't know anything. You are an empty vessel. The gig is up. You can't think of one thought. There are no thoughts. It's over. You're doomed.
11. Check out Buzzfeed.
12. Look up your latest symptoms on WebMD. Feel sad about your obvious onset of kidney failure and/or scoliosis. Might be rectal cancer. A little hazy still. But clearly terminal.
13. Clean the baseboards in your office. This cannot wait. You

cannot work in these conditions. It is unsanitary. All of a sudden, you can just see them. They are offensive and harming your mojo.

14. Lunchtime.
15. Short nap.
16. Kids are home.
17. Package up your shame and try again tomorrow.

HOW TO GET YOUR CHILD TO POOP ON THE POTTY

1. Be confident. You are a smart, educated woman not to be outwitted by tiny humans.
2. Use your God-given creativity to carefully construct a sticker chart. Hang chart. You are amazing. You have a system.
3. Buy bribes (chocolate chips, M&Ms, Skittles). Go ahead and eat some. You deserve it.
4. Lovingly explain your plan to toddler. Watch him take in your wisdom. See him hearing you. Parenting is a beautiful exchange.
5. Implement plan. Be strong.

Day 1—You are Mama Warrior. That chart will be full of stickers in no time. You will be giving lessons on this soon. This is going on Pinterest.

Day 7—You're wearing down. Chin up, buttercup. All the screaming is worth your new phase of toddler underwear. This battle surely only has two or three days left in it.

Day 19—You are singing "I believe I can fly" outside the door of the bathroom, because that makes sense somehow. You are ever so slightly coming unhinged. You refuse to offer another pull-up so he can poop in it in the corner. This is not your life. You went to college. You were president of the Honor Society. How are you getting bested by a three-year-old's intestines? You are a smart person. People love you. Your days used to make sense. You used to wear pants with a button.

Day 52—I see you over there crying, eating all the M&Ms. Just throw a pull-up on him and call it a day. Maybe he'll give it up by middle school. You don't care.

HOW TO HAVE FAMILY DEVOTIONAL AT DINNER

1. Emotionally invest in high hopes. This is key. Envision a sacred family moment. Prepare to feel sentimental. Crushed expectations are an important part of this.
2. At the onset of dinner, immediately break up several sibling fights while husband plays Candy Crush.
3. With thinning patience, begin carefully selected family devo. Get interrupted several times, because there's not enough ketchup, where's more bread, does this have onions in it, can I have orange juice instead of water, his elbow keeps touching me, no offense but this is kind of boring.
4. Field questions about a sleepover Friday, an ortho appointment, armpit hair, and a new data plan.
5. Take deep breaths. Act like you're teaching Sunday school. You are so interesting. You aren't having rage issues while talking about Moses.
6. Imagine that your family is totally into this. They are not, but imagine it.
7. Finally lose your crap like a raging maniac. Slam devotional book on dinner table, screaming, "Forget it! Just hate God!"

while family stares at you like you're a crazy person because you actually are.

8. Watch husband roll eyes and pour you Pinot Grigio. Eat your cold dinner in shame.

Programming Note: Successful family devos are an important event in The Contest (see chapter 3). You may just sit this event out rather than drop in the rankings.

HOW TO CHOOSE THE CORRECT COLOR PALETTE FOR YOUR PRESCHOOLER

1. Don't. You will be wrong.

HOW TO CHOOSE THE CORRECT PROM DRESS, FRIEND, CLASS, BOYFRIEND, GIRLFRIEND, SWEATPANTS, HAIRCUT, MUSIC, JOB, BEDSPREAD, LIFE PATH FOR YOUR TEENAGER

1. Don't. You will be wrong.

HOW TO DO LAUNDRY

1. Separate lights and darks. This is the best you can do. I guess the reds and blues go with the black shirts, and the gray stuff goes with the lights. I don't know, man. Wonder why you bought all these clothes for people.
2. Put lights in washing machine and start.

3. Remember this load two days later.
4. Rewash the lights that now smell like a filthy neighborhood pool lined with mold.
5. Remember them the next day. Laundry is hard. Don't feel bad about yourself.
6. Wash a third time, and add bleach to counter the mildew-soaked fibers that are semipermanent now.
7. Put lights in the dryer and start the darks.
8. Remember the darks! Yay you! Despair at the light load in the dryer. This is like discovering the dishes in the dishwasher are clean. Throw the load of lights on your bed to "fold in a few minutes" while you move the darks to the dryer.
9. Co-sleep with the light load that night. Give them their own bed space, like a person. Bonus: they can double as an extra pillow and blanket!
10. The next morning, move lights to the floor to "fold later today," and proceed to step over them until next Tuesday. Make sure to get some of the dirty clothes you take off mixed in with the pile.
11. Pull dark clothes as necessary out of the dryer for the next five days, one item at a time.

Programming Note: If this laundry situation causes you to go on a rage bender one day, like an asylum escapee, perhaps your husband could adopt the Brandon Hatmaker Approach and emergency purchase four color-coded baskets per family member correlating with an elaborate laundry system he invented on the dash to Walmart, and if you specialize in math, you realize that a well-timed meltdown might result in your spouse doubling down with twenty-eight laundry baskets. We don't play in this family.

Grown don't mean *nothing* to a mother. A child is a child. They get bigger, older, but grown? In my *heart* it don't mean a thing.[1]

–TONI MORRISON

CHAPTER 22

STRING EIGHTEEN PARTIES TOGETHER

Allow me to share last night's dinner conversation courtesy of the "4th Grade Public School Puberty Talk" starring girls in one room with their teacher and boys in the gym with the coach:

REMY: Ben, you are going to get the puberties too.

BEN: I've already started!

REMY: You got your period?

BEN: Oh my gosh. No. I am getting pit hair, and my muscles are getting awesome.

REMY: Periods mean we have babies. I think they come out of our butt.

SYDNEY: No, they don't, Remy! You don't poop out babies.

REMY: Well, girls have three holes, and they come out of one of them.

BEN: WHAT? Girls have three holes? My friend was right!

SYDNEY: You have two of them, Ben!

BEN: I know. We pee out of our eureka.

SYDNEY: It's a urethra!

REMY: Puberties means we get hair on our privates.

BEN: Our health class video was animated, and it
     zoomed in on the penis and one by one, hair started
     popping out. Pop, pop, pop! I heard you get hair on
     your nipples.

SYDNEY: Ben, I bet you were born with a lot of hair.

BEN: On my nipples?

SYDNEY: Oh my gosh.

REMY: Do moms have hair on their nipples when they
     feed their babies?

BEN: Gross! The babies get hair in their mouths?

REMY: It's the puberties.

LORDT. We are obviously raising children with basic bio-logical competency. (This table talk was sponsored by Cabernet Sauvignon.)

It is raining teenagers in the Hatmaker house: we have one in college, two in high school, one in middle, and one lone innocent in elementary. We are in a completely different parenting space than we were ten years ago, when my days revolved around pre-school, playdates, and the Kids Eat Free website (sincere apologies to Kerbey Lane where kids ate free on Tuesdays and my friends and I brought eleven children; it was less a *dining experience* and more an *invasion*).

Now we are dealing with sex, porn, social media, young adulthood, college, financial solvency, deep questions of faith, the puberties. Good times! It is so real up in here. Our oldest just fin-ished his first year at Texas Tech University and the second leaves next fall, so we are not messing around anymore. The entire thing happened just like the people said it would. Every year on their birthdays, they actually turn a whole year older; string eighteen parties together, and they move into a college dorm. It's absurd.

Parenting teens is exactly what I thought it would be and nothing like I thought it would be. I was prepared for parts of it, and may I begin with those, specifically for my young mamas still in the twilight zone of wishing your children would just go pee-pee on the freaking potty while simultaneously dreading the end of early childhood. It is a strange dichotomy, the trying to "enjoy every moment" while sometimes locking yourself in the bathroom with old Halloween candy and pretending you can't hear them. Add to that dissociative disorder the older mamas *insisting* you enjoy toddlerhood because it is all crap from here: "Oh, you think a temper tantrum is hard? Wait until your junior throws a kegger while you are at a sales convention." Um. Thank you?

In my experience, parenting teens is easily the best phase of motherhood yet. To be fair, I'm geared toward older kids, and my parents loved having teenagers (which made us love *being* their teenagers), so I had a precedent to enjoy this stage. But all that withstanding, big kids are fun. They really are. Yours will be too. Text with my oldest:

ME: Where are you?
HIM: Doing drugs with gangs.
ME: Don't share needles.

Teens are hilarious and interesting and smart; plus, I was made to nurture independence, which they want so bad they can taste it. I'm not a natural hoverer or worrier, so pushing them toward maturity is not where I struggle. I have no problem letting the chips fall where they may, letting them feel the sting of their own choices or the gut punch of failure, because those are the very best teachers. The flip side is owning their own successes, forging their own path, and let me tell you: when your kid handles every last scrap of paperwork, applications, interviews, and scholarship entries and lands his college acceptance letters singlehandedly, he confidently steps toward adulthood, and *you love this for him.*

I planned on adoring the teen years, so I do.

Watching your kids grow into young adults in front of your eyes is truly breathtaking. Mostly good, sometimes not. They have big-time issues now, some you never saw coming, others you were positively insulated from except that you weren't, some that will break your heart right alongside theirs. They fall in love, they put their vulnerable souls in the hands of untrustworthy people, they worry more than they let on, they mess up epically, dramatically, shockingly. They lie and then act wounded when you double-check: *Hand over that phone, Miss Hurt Feelings. I was sixteen once. My mom thought I was at Stacy's.*

So don't hear me say the teenage years are always a dreamy dream or, heaven forbid, that I love these years because my teens are all well-mannered missionaries-in-training. For the love, mine are pastor's kids, so they are predisposed to, say, for instance, "vape" with a friend in the bathroom at a football game and land two days of detention. (My girlfriend: "Vaping? Ugh. I'd be less concerned that he was an addict and more concerned he is just an ass.")

Side note: it is incredibly helpful to have girlfriends who aren't too precious about this phase. If your friends clutch their pearls at every teen wobble, it is like booking yourself a first-class ticket on the Failure Train. Trust me: you want truth-telling friends raising normal teens in the real world. If another mom tells you she is certain *her* teenage son has never even *considered* porn (oh dear), you may want to de-board because this might not be a safe or honest place for real life. Yes, we maintain solid expectations for our teens, but they are normal kids just like we were, and they will screw up just like we did, and our tribe needs to handle this stage with solidarity and grace, not shock and superiority. If you want judgment, call your mom.

The Hatmakers have real stuff going on well beyond e-cigarettes, and we've failed each other more than I thought possible these last few years, but I am here to tell you the teen years are not to be feared or approached with dread. Even better, face them with joy! There is no formula for sailing through this parenting stage. No template works in every family, no list of rules will prevent catastrophe, no one story is exactly like the next. But I can tell you a tiny handful of truths that have carried the Hatmaker clan thus far and still left us liking each other.

We promised our kids early and often: You can tell us anything. We won't freak out. You can't shock us. Nothing is a deal breaker, and everything is up for discussion. We primed the pump by broaching plenty of sticky conversations ourselves:

- Who is already having sex in your grade?
- What about God do you have trouble believing?
- How do you and your gay friends talk about sexuality?
- What do you struggle with?
- What have you heard lately that you don't understand?
- What questions do you have about your own body?

Obviously these questions are met with deer-in-the-headlights paralysis sometimes, but our kids have no doubt we meant what we said; we clearly aren't afraid of any conversation, any subject, any issue. We removed the cloak of silence that often suffocates hard topics, and with it went much of the corollary angst. For many teens, the hardest thing imaginable is even *talking* to their parents about real life, so once they do and discover that no one dies, it paves the road for all sorts of dialogue. Don't wait for them to make the first move here, because teens are notoriously secretive and weird.

Then is the follow-up of actually not freaking out. If you could hear the things our ears have heard in this house while managing to not fall out of our chairs, you would nominate us for awards and prizes and parades. Sometimes your brain has to tell your face to pull it together while your adrenaline loses its crap invisibly. You want to shut down communication? Fall apart, scream, overreact, shun. When you have no earthly idea how to respond yet, just say: "Tell me more about that," or "I'm listening and need a bit of time to think about this," or "I'm glad you told me, and we will work this out together." Keep it open, keep it mutual, stay on the same team instead of isolating your kid. Our teens need to know that we are *for them* and *with them,* not just when they are performing well but in struggle, failure, calamity. This is, after all, exactly how God loves us.

Brandon and I also took a page out of my parents' handbook and decided to have fun with our bigs. We laugh, we tease, we joke, we tell funny stories, we send ridiculous memes. Determined to be the destination for teen fun, when parks and children's museums ran their course, we bought a used boat and guaranteed ten more years of loyalty. We virtually never say no to their friends coming over. Loving your teens means loving their friends, and the formula is easy: feed them constantly and ask good questions about their lives. The end. Be the home where the teen tribe is welcomed, and you'll rack up credits quicker than expanding their data plan.

We permanently opened the yes valve on teen shenanigans that hover north of dumb but south of harmful. Fill up the back of your truck with an inflatable swimming pool and drive around the neighborhood? Sure. Host a mancathalon in the backyard with events like Eating Hot Peppers and Trampoline Volleyball?

We have insurance. Unless we have a strong reason otherwise, we say *yes*, thrilled they are mudding in a pasture instead of sneaking out of a super-restrictive home. Can they ruin this freedom? You bet, and they have to earn it back over time, but our relationship thrives better when the reins are clearly in place but not pulled too tight.

Perhaps no parenting stage requires levity more than raising young adults. If you can, at every turn, in any circumstance possible, *lighten up*. This season is a blink, a tiny bitty handful of years in an entire lifetime in which our children have lost their ever-lovin' minds (to be more exact, their minds are under-developed and impaired; it's the puberties). It is a millisecond and then it is over, and we surely don't want to damage our relationships beyond repair during these few years our kids struggle through the painful process of growing up. We can hold the line knowing full well they will not always roll their eyes, come home late, lie to our faces, or sulk like it is their job. In a New York minute they will be grown-ups, and just like we did, they will look back on these years with laughter and plenty of face palms, remembering parents who stuck by them and with them, daresay even enjoyed them despite it all.

Expect to love these years, and even when they are hard, you will.

I, for one, was hanging on to my son's ankles, barely believing his time under our roof was over. It went so fast. Everyone was right. After moving him into his dorm, I clung to that boy at the airport curb and thought I might never breathe a full, deep breath again. Launching the baby that made me a mother sliced our story in half: when I raised him and when he left. I cried the whole way home. Why do they have to go to college right when they get the most awesome? Why can't we send our kids to college between fourth and seventh grade? (Kidding. Well, I'm mostly kidding.)

These are the kids of my dreams, and I like them so much. I cannot believe we got to raise them. Their teen years have brought me more joy than I dared imagine. These hooligans are both exactly what I expected and beyond what I hoped for, because who really knew what kind of humans they would turn into? I had an inkling, but then they develop into these amazing, nuanced, better versions of your early caricature, and you realize that they are whole, complete people with bits of you and lots of them and, as it turns out, they belong to God after all. When they were little, I said, "They are on loan from God," but I didn't really mean it because it seemed like they actually belonged to me and would forever, but then one enrolls in college seven hours away and it becomes painfully and awesomely clear: *Oh my gosh. There he actually goes. Bye, baby.*

They are going after all, mamas. Let's send them off adored, believed in, enjoyed, treasured, lest they forget that until our last breath, our doors are always open, our tables will always be full of food, their people are welcomed with open arms, and no matter what they say, they will always be ours.

Although the world
is full of *suffering*,
it is also full of the
 of it.[1]

–HELEN KELLER

ℓℓ

CHAPTER 23

REWOVEN

Matching my mother-in-law's comprehensive skill set is a thing that will happen to me never. She can do pretty much anything: garden, cook, fish, cross-stitch, golf. She started a food pantry. She knows everything about accounting. She knows everything about holistic oncology. She knows everything about tax codes. She lived in Europe. She lived in Hawaii. Perhaps this simple sentence will help you understand: Jacki once went on a four-day elk hunt in the Rocky Mountains in the dead of winter, shot an elk, then skinned, quartered (is this the word?), and packed the animal down the mountain alone *on her horse*. She also made my sister-in-law's wedding dress by hand, because don't all horseback elk hunters also sew?

In addition to doing everything, she crocheted custom baby blankets for all her grandchildren. These are heirlooms that we all cherish. Jacki made a particularly complicated and elaborate blanket for my daughter Sydney, and when she was still little, our dog at the time, Satan's own mongrel, went absolutely Tasmanian devil on it and tried to bury it in the backyard. The blanket was destroyed.

I was beside myself. I picked up the tattered yarn and sobbed at the dog, "THIS IS WHY WE CAN'T HAVE NICE THINGS!" I delivered the pile of slobbery, filthy yarn shreds to Jacki to see if anything could be done, because sure, she could make a replacement replica, but *these were the threads that covered my sleeping baby girl.* I didn't want a new blanket; I wanted the old one put back together.

Jacki washed the shredded yarn pile by hand, sorted out all the tangles and knots, and slowly, tenderly, over weeks and weeks, put the blanket back together, slightly different than before but using all the same threads. "Bonus," she told me, "it's actually sturdier than it originally was, so you can wash it in the machine now!"

Put a pin in that story. We'll come back to it.

God's sovereignty. (I know. Where is this little narrative going? Stick with me for three more minutes.) I have a thorny relationship with the concept of God's sovereignty, this spiritual idea that God is entirely controlling all things at all times in all circumstances, that nothing happens without His say-so, nothing occurs outside of His decree. This discussion in spiritual circles often confuses me. Maybe it is just the semantics, primarily a function of the language used or perhaps the words left out. It probably has something to do with living longer, seeing more, and diversifying my exposure, which challenges my doctrine.

Either way, I have to overcome my anxiety at being placed outside the camp here for asking these questions—belonging is a serious bedfellow of mine. But then I remember what Bob Goff said on Twitter about camps: *"God didn't give us anything to join, except Him."* If we're doing this thing right, the family can stay intact through hard questions, disagreements, and a severe wrestle with divine mysteries.

Questions like: Why do really heinous things happen to really innocent people? Why does God intervene in some circumstances but not in others? Why does praying in faith not heal everyone? What do faith and prayer even mean? If God is going to do what He wants, then why doesn't He fix more stuff? And why do we even need to pray? Do our prayers move God? If they do, it doesn't feel like He is that sovereign if human people can change His mind. If God is in control of absolutely everything, does sin have any real effect? Does Satan have any real effect? Is there *any* factor that can operate outside of God's sovereignty? What does it mean, "He allowed suffering"? How do we understand God when He stays His hand in the face of injustice or abuse?

Sometimes it seems like God can either be sovereign or benevolent but not both.

Isn't this such a light little conversation?

If those questions made you feel faint, I'll say this: I am no longer afraid of spiritual investigation. I'm confident in the end game, which is that God is good and He loves us and He could not possibly be unfair, arbitrary, cold, or abusive. He couldn't be. It is outside the possibility of His character. It isn't just that God is loving but that *He is love itself.* I am so certain of that. I possess full confidence in God but a healthy skepticism of the human understanding of God. (I used to be the opposite, and I miss the days when I knew everything.) So in this case, I can see the clear answer at the end of the problem and realize I simply don't understand the equation. I know the final answer is right, but I haven't worked out the spiritual math.

Back to the questions.

With anything as viscerally devastating as suffering and all its messy appendages, it is difficult to explore thoroughly without unintentionally becoming dismissive. But, still, the Christian community has long tried to explain it. We want to understand

God's role because it goes to the heart of His character, which goes to the heart of our perceived belovedness. At its core, the question boils down to: Am I just a bit part in the greater story of God's glory? Or am I truly a loved daughter?

What we typically want to know when tragedy strikes is *why*. It is hard to reconcile arbitrary suffering with a loving God, isn't it? We want an unambiguous explanation instead of the mysterious cocktail of sovereignty, the common human experience, God's glory, and redemption.

To this end, the church has a history of formulizing suffering, giving it tidier origins and endings, and whitewashing the debilitating middle. We assess the complicated nuances of sorrow and assign it categories, roots, principles. Or, uncertain, we default to sovereignty in a way that feels so lonely and cold, it makes God out to be a heartless pursuer of His own fame at any human cost. That just feels gross.

Here is what we know about suffering from Scripture:

- Sometimes people suffer because of self-inflicted misery and sin. Humans have long been their own worst enemies. We are a self-destructive people who prefer to blame. *Adam, Eve, Jonah, David, Saul, Judas.*
- Sometimes people suffer because of the sins of others, which God would never cause, endorse, or initiate. It is contrary to his perfect nature. *Bathsheba, Daniel, Tamar, Hosea, the beaten man in the Good Samaritan story, Paul.*
- Sometimes people suffer through no human fault at all. The best of God's saints had their dark nights. This is no indicator of divine disfavor. Life is simply hard.
- Sometimes people suffer specifically for the gospel, which the Bible said we would.
- Sometimes people suffer because loved ones get sick and

die. This happens to every person, family, and community on earth. Even Jesus wept salty, human tears at death and the grief of his friends.

- Sometimes people suffer because we live on a physical earth involving tornadoes, earthquakes, wildfires, tsunamis. Natural disasters are a part of any living, shifting, fluctuating planet. (And the longer we irresponsibly plunder and harm it, the greater it will groan and creak and protest, but that is a different essay.)
- Sometimes people suffer because we have a vicious enemy who hates us and is out to steal, kill, and destroy everything redemptive and beautiful. That is real.

The point is, there is no formula for suffering. There is no one answer. There is no pat explanation. Scripture clearly identifies numerous root causes of suffering, some entirely incompatible with God's character. Because He is so good at being God, He uses everything, He can heal anything, He wrestles glory from all things. Paradoxically, adversity can be so good for us, and He knows that. So regardless of why or how life delivers pain, God makes the absolute most of it.

Back to Sydney's shredded baby blanket.

In Genesis 50, Joseph told his brothers after they sold him into slavery in a fit of jealous rage (WTH, brothers?): "You meant evil against me, but God meant it for good . . ." This is important: *Meant* is the Hebrew word for *wove*. In other words, you wove evil but God rewove it together for good. After his brothers went Tasmanian devil on him and essentially tried to bury him in the backyard, Joseph deposited all the tattered shreds of his life into the careful hands of God, who just picked up the threads of hate and deceit and abandonment and injustice and refashioned them into a truly beautiful story.

God used all the same threads. He didn't create a replica. He didn't start from scratch. He didn't throw the destroyed original in the trash and begin again with all new material. God rewove what was torn into a stronger version than the first.

This is a perfect depiction of sovereignty to me. He is Lord over all, no matter how it began, how it was meant, how it harmed. He reigns over intent, over agenda, over loss. Nothing escapes His reach, nothing is beyond reclamation in His hands. If someone or something sewed threads of suffering in your life, even if that someone was you, God's sovereignty says: *I'm bigger than that, stronger than that, more powerful than that. I can make this beautiful again and use it to heal you and make you sturdier and, while we're at it, other people too.* At its most altruistic, loving center, God is indeed glorified through our suffering, not because He is an egomaniac who profits from our losses, but because, truly, nothing bears a better witness than watching God resurrect someone's life. That is a God who folks want to know, a God worth His glory.

So in the face of brokenheartedness, there's no need to counsel people in the way of spiritual explanation, for we are guessing at best, misrepresenting God at worst. Nor should we push them into tidy grief. God will reweave the threads in time—the approximate gap between Joseph's brothers selling him into slavery and him standing before them as the second-highest leader in the country: twenty-two years. We don't need to hustle others through their stories. Or ourselves.

Here is what we can cling to:

- God is impossibly loving. He loves us. He loves our families. He loves creation.
- God restores things; all of history points to a God who makes sad things right.

- God is very much paying attention. He is on the move—healing and transforming. He can do this. This is what He does.
- There is nothing too broken that God cannot mend and redeem. Really. Nothing.
- God doesn't tempt, abuse, endorse wickedness, abandon, or hate. Let's not lay evils at His feet that don't belong to Him.
- For all of history, God has used suffering to make us stronger, even when it was born of sin, failure, injustice, or abuse. It is not wasted. It can even be precious.
- When we are crushed, Jesus is as close as our own skin. He suffered greatly, and we are molded more into His image when we share that spiritual space. There is a Jesus maturity only available to us in suffering. It's true.
- He has given us to one another as agents of love and grace and safety.
- He told us hundreds of times to comfort each other, making sure we are cared for.
- Jesus wept over death and grief; shed your tears, friend. We have a Savior who cries.
- It is not our responsibility to explain why. We are family. We circle the wagons. We make casseroles. We weep with those who weep.

Suffering invites us to be radically human with one another, perhaps doing nothing more than reaching across the table, clasping hands, and crying together. We are afforded the chance to create a safe place for someone to mourn; nothing is needed but space, proximity, presence, empathy. Grief cannot be sidestepped; it must be endured. May we be a people who endure with one another well, slow to formulize and quick to empathize, because life is so very hard and until God reweaves all things, people are dying for a cold cup of water in their pain.

As for those sovereignty questions, I am sorry to say I don't exactly understand how it all works this side of heaven. I'm just not sure. It is too complicated and nuanced and interwoven and not at all prescriptive (all the formulas dissolve under scrutiny). I can tell you what I make of the end game—I believe God's sovereignty ultimately means He will have it all back. Every wrong will eventually be right. Every injustice will be overturned. Every tear will be dried. All the torn pieces will be rewoven. Every prayer utilized to bring us another inch closer to Jesus and more in partnership with His love. This earth and realm will be repossessed into glory, and God will have the world He dreamed of. Some redemption will be in our lifetime, and all of it will be in eternity.

Sovereignty means none of this is too far gone; nothing is outside God's ultimate plans. No matter how off the rails this world appears, God's eye has always been on the tiny, fragile sparrow. He has never lost count of an injustice, a life, a human being. No nameless death was ever nameless. No senseless abuse was ever missed. He may have set the whole earth in motion with its mix of humanity and spiritual realms and principalities, but only One is on the throne where He has always been and will always be. If we are still holding a pile of tattered threads, it just means the story is not over yet.

We can trust God entirely until heaven when He vanquishes all tears, all death, all mourning, all crying, all pain, and He reigns and He won and He fixed it all and saved it all and restored it all.

Grace and peace and mercy to you in the beautiful reweaving.

ONE MORE WORD
AS YOU GO . . .

Yesterday, I was at level nine hundred crankiness. A combination of factors really: some online drama, a hard week in the news, a bit of travel fatigue, this relentless heat (go home, Austin, you're drunk), and a general sense that the whole world is a mess and nothing will ever go right again and no one loves anyone and we are all doomed. No big deal. I'm not overreacting; YOU'RE overreacting.

Anyhow, savvy to my own red flags, I did what I always do when I'm careening toward a meltdown: I called my best friends. Well, let's at least tell the truth—I *texted* them (I try to use my phone for actual phone calls never). I sent an SOS text lamenting "a cloud of yuck over my head" and asked them to come over for Happy Hour to sit on my porch together and fix me.

They showed up at 5:30 and left at 11:15.

We ate Chips and Salsa Dinner, and everything got put back together. As is usually the case, the yuck cloud had been hovering over all of us in big or small ways, so once again, the "me too" factor was healing in and of itself. And then, of course, all the other magical tools: Prosecco, cheese, funny stories, a few demonstrations of our most absurd yoga poses, picking up the fallen yogi after failing to master the "locust scorpion," the kids running around the yard, fresh air, Chris Stapleton on the speakers, God in us and among us and for us.

Today, I'm thinking of you. Thank you for thumbing through all the previous pages and spending time with me here. I do not take your time and loyalty and love lightly. When I think of our tribe, the one you and I along with so many others have built, I think of girlfriends on the porch. I think of SOS texts and friends at the ready and laughter and a few tears and togetherness. Always the togetherness. Last night was a picture-perfect description of how I'd describe this community of women: all the mess, because we tell the truth, and all the moxie, because telling the truth sets us free.

I imagine you barefoot on my porch with a crisp glass of Prosecco paired with chips, because we aren't fancy. I imagine you telling me outrageous and amazing stories of all your Bonus Moms and how they've loved you and rescued you. I'd like to hear your tales of renovations gone wonky and that one time you painted your kitchen fluorescent green because you were in a real mood. I bet you have your own version of the Private Baby brother story, and you can probably match my Driving Accidentally to San Antonio for a Field Trip gaffe, because motherhood is basically *humility training*. We could talk for days about how exercise is trying to kill us and would obviously devote a whole night to our favorite Netflix shows.

I also know you could absolutely identify with my stories of heartbreak and broken bodies and hurting kids and dreams gone sideways. I know you could, because you've told me. We've endured much. Sanctuary, Forgiveness School, the Cabin, the Grocery Store—you get my places; you have your own versions that are holy and hard and hilarious. No one came to these pages unscathed; we are learning and unlearning and figuring out what to hold on to and what to release. Sometimes life is great and sometimes it is painful beyond recognition, and yet here we all are: still standing.

Still standing.

We have breath in our lungs: still standing. We have people who love us: still standing. We have a God who spends all His hours making broken things whole again: still standing. We are smart and resilient and so very funny and capable, and the days ahead of us stretch unwritten, unsullied, untarnished: still standing. That's our moxie. We have everything we need.

Sure, these are some of my stories, but really, they are all our stories. They encompass big dreams and home and Jesus and motherhood and childhood memories and husbands and our own parents and church and struggle and triumph. These are ours. And I want you to know I hold your versions with tender hands—in the ways they are similar to mine and in the ways they are polar opposite. Some of you didn't have healthy parents, and the love note to mine was painful to read. I hold that space for you with great affection. Some of you aren't married or you're divorced, and the husband and wife parts in here felt distant or raw. Listen, you may not be a wife, but we are still sisters. I'd previously titled one of the essays "Hiding in the Car Eating Crackers" since sometimes moms can be found doing such scandalous things, and my editor Jessica, who doesn't have children, wrote back: "I've never in my life hidden in the car eating crackers. I don't even get this." I howled. Mom Life is so weird.

You have some gorgeous and difficult variations, and this is what makes us stronger together. You are vibrant in areas where I'm weak, and you bring a perspective to the table that the rest of us absolutely cannot live without. You offer depth and nuance and perception to every conversation we share, and the tribe is immeasurably better for it. I am immeasurably better for it. I've learned so much from you. You are precious to me, and I count you among my life's greatest treasure. I sincerely mean that.

So let's go forth, Moxie Ladies. We have a world to love and a sisterhood to expand, and we're just the girls for the job.

FOREVER YOUR FANGIRL,

Jen

Acknowledgments

I want to thank my readers first. I cannot imagine a more loyal, loving, hilarious community of (mostly) women. We have been through so much together, and I envision your faces with every word I write. This is for you, all of it, because I love you sincerely. Thank you for being so good to me. My only mission is to serve you well.

Launch Team: you are, as you know, my people. From a rag-tag group of strangers pulled together to launch *For the Love* in January 2015 to what I can only describe as our own little church, my devotion is absolute and forever. Our FTL babies, parties, meet-ups, trips, groups, merch, that time we bought one of our own a car, that time we helped send one of our own to college, . . . you are every good thing. You have all the mess and all the moxie and I adore you. You've convinced me the community I've always dreamed of is possible.

My team at Thomas Nelson means more to me than I can figure out how to say. Brian Hampton, Jeff James, Karen Jackson, Tiffany Sawyer, Aryn VanDyke, Janene MacIvor, Heather Skelton, my editor Jessica Wong—your belief in me, the way you let me be me, absorbing my suggestion that the cover design include a pin-up girl without laughing in my face, our many, many hours around the table and on twilight cruise—you are my publishing home where I feel safe, loved, and welcomed. And Jessica, this book is so different from the first version I sent you, because you are a brilliant, persnickety, obsessive editor. You made it so much better. SO MUCH. My readers should send you flowers. Thank you. I love you, Team.

All my love and loyalty to Heather Adams, Beth Gebhard, and Kerry Gardner of Choice Media and Communications. For two projects in a row, plus all the in-between, you've gone well beyond the call of duty as smart, savvy publicists. Well beyond. You are sisters, collaborators, cheerleaders, and travel partners, including that time we took an "Uber" on a snowy day in New York City, and it was just some random guy driving a Camaro. Good times, girls. Love you dearly.

I cannot possibly, remotely imagine where I would be without my agent, Curtis Yates, and his wife and my favorite reader, Karen (love you forever for the gecko with mouth rot story), and our partner in crime, Mike Salisbury. Someone recently spoke about our relationship and said something about "just business" and I about came undone. You are far more than "just business" partners. Curtis, you are like the most overprotective brother a girl could ever want, and I love you for it. Thank you for the *years* you've guided and stood beside me. I am the most grateful girl. You are so important to me.

To my assistant, Amanda Duckett, I cannot even think of my life without you. Nothing would be done, e-mailed, edited, composed, booked, confirmed, scanned, considered, developed, or accomplished. You and I both know this is true. Your ability to work with an impulsive, unorganized, Big Idea Girl without losing your mind will surely get you straight into heaven. Your ability to speak for me, predict what I need, and communicate on my behalf is so uncanny, it is as if we share the same brain (except yours is organized and systematic and does all the real thinking). I love you, sister.

This is the first book in which I included a few stories about my first family, the one I grew up in. Mom, Dad, Lindsay, Cortney, and Drew: the best, the funniest, the loudest, the tightest, the most obnoxious, the most protective, and the most amazing. You are my safest place, the people I always want, always reach for. We were overloved and overvalued and we don't even care. Just think: one day we'll inherit Grandma's mink, and God willing, the red horse trailer that refuses to go down without a fight. I love you. Our family is what family should feel like.

I can't not create line space on this page for my A.S.S.S. sisters (don't ask). Girls, everything. That is what we've been through and shared. Everything. Every single thing. Your voices of love and hilarity are constantly in my ears (literally), and I love you so much, I could just freak out. You are true sisters, and I trust you and adore you and need you and would take a bullet for you.

Gavin, Sydney, Caleb, Ben, and Remy: When I dreamed about becoming a mom, I didn't have one hot clue what that would actually mean. But now I know: it means thinking about you basically every minute of every day, sneaking in to see you sleep at night, watching you across rooms and barely believing that you are mine. Fine, sometimes it also means stalking you on Instagram. If I could handpick five kids in the entire universe to raise, it would be you five. Dad and I are just crazy about you. Watching you grow up into young adults right now is the most amazing, shocking, beautiful thing.

And finally, to Brandon, married twenty-four years this December. I don't think anyone on earth could love me like you do. I have always felt seen and known and cared for inside our marriage, and that is a true gift. We're on the downhill slope here on this parenting gig, which is exciting and terrible. But I know I can anticipate an amazing new chapter with you after we've wrapped this part up, because I like you and we're awesome together. Let's travel. Let's move into a loft. Let's get new tattoos. Let's sit on a lot of porches and beaches and docks and toast this little life of ours. Thanks for being my person. I love you.

My Wild and Glorious Launch Team

Kim Adam
Heather Adams
Amanda Alcamo
Bethany Alexander
Robin Allen
Anne Alley
Laine Alves
Mary Anderle
Mitzi Arellano
Elizabeth Arnold
Heather Averill
Darla Baerg
Erica Bailey
Morgan Baker
Allison Ball
Courtney Banceu
Rachel Bardgett
Ashlee Barlow
Celeste Barnard
Parker Barnes
Christan Barnett
Megan Barnett
Amber Barrett
Lisa Bartelt
Erin Bassett
Cindy Battles
Christy Beach
Amber Beamer-Rohde
Bethany Beams

Chaselynn Beard
Georgette Beck
Rebecca Beckett
Connie Beckham
Kelly Becktold
Emily Bedwell
Ashley Behn
Jennifer Bell
Ashley Besser
Kodi BeVelle
Sue Bidstrup
Emma Bircher
Courtney Birkbeck
Stephanie Bishop
Amanda Boardman
Jennifer Bond
Miriam Boone
Kresta Bosley
Catherine Bost
Kaitlyn Bouchillon
Christine Bowin
Jenna Boyd
Angela Bradford
Heather Brady
Lindsay Brandon-Smith
Sarah Bratt
Erin Brazofsky
Kandice Bridges
Danielle Bright

Cindy Brill
Dyan Bronstein
Danielle Brower
Amanda Brown
Jamie Brown
Theresa Brown
Jane Brummett
Sarah Buckel
Kelly Buddenhagen
Kelly Buist
Kristen Bulgrien
Ashley Bunnell
Lynn Burdine
Elizabeth Burnfield
Jessica Burrows
Clare Butler
Hidi Byrd
Megan Byrd
Liv Campbell
April Cao
Sue Carbajal
Ashley Carbonatto
Hannah Card
Leslie Carlton
Wanda Carlton
Anna Carpenter
Nichole Carrabbia
Angela Carroll
Shellie Carson
Amanda Carver
Nicole Case

Regina Chari
Chelsia Checkal
Tomi Cheeks
Kristin Cheng
Mindy Christianson
Katie Ciccione
Jenniemarie Cisneros
Becky Clark
Corie Clark
Elise Cleary
Stephanie Clinton
Miranda Coker
Jess Collier
Andrea Conway
Bridgette Cook
Brenda Cordova
Ann Marie Corgill
Whitney Cornelison
Monica Cornell
Erin Cox
Wendy Cox
Vickie Cozad
Kylee Craggett
Melissa Crawford
Heather Crespim
Colleen Crocker
Mary Cumberledge
Angelica Czubkowski
Amy Dail

ACKNOWLEDGMENTS

Angie Dailey
Heather Danek
Laura Daniels
Robin Dauma
Cathy Davidson
Amy Davis
Athena Davis
Cassie Davis
Tara Davis
Rebecca Degeilh
Suzanne DeLaney
Alyssa
DeLosSantos
Danielle DeWitt
Jennifer Dickey
Nicole Diehl
Amy Dieter-Decker
Eryn Dillion
Meleah Dillion
Molly Dixon
Grace Dobson
April Dobson
Emily Donehoo
Lauren Douglas
Brandi Dowdy
Terra Doyle
Stacey Drake
Amanda Duckett
Christina Duncan
Jennifer Early
Erin Earnest
Carlee Easton
Brandi-lin Ebersole
Amy Edgar
Mandy
Edmondson
Andi Edwards
Katie Eller
Laura Elliott
Stephenie Ellis
Emily Engle
Rachael Ennis
Katy Epling

Lindsay Evans
Leah Evanson
Kelly Fain
Bekah Fairley
Terry Felix
Mrs FishGuy
Lauren Flake
Kara Flathouse
Cydney Fletcher
Jodi Fletchet
Nichole Forbes
Codie Forman
Michelle Fortik
Brooke Fradd
Barbara Fritz
Carol Fruge
Terri Fullerton
Jennifer Gardner
Kerry Gardner
Holly Garin
Ashley Garrett
Jenny Garwood
Jen Gash
Beth Gates
Amy Gatlin
Kiah Geleynse
Brianna George
Heidi Gerson
Heather Gerwing
Lauren Gibbins
Corie Gibbs
Kathryn Giese
Anne Gift
Lindsey Gipson
Ann Goade
Marci Godfroy
Jen Goforth
Vicki Gordillo Watt
Nicki Gorney
Angela Gottschalk
Krista Gradias
Heather Grady
Karen Graham

Angela Graves
Rebecca Greebon
Carey Gregg
Ashley Griffin
Brittany Griffin
Nova Grimm
Gina Grizzle
Erica Groen
Elizabeth
Grossman
Amy Guthrie
Amanda Gutierrez
Sue Hall
Kassi Hamilton
Jessica Hamlet
Laura Hamrick
Kendra Hanson
Harmony Harkema
Carolyn Harper
Lora Hartwell
Nanette Haskin
Jodi Hatmaker
Jennifer Hayes
Kelly Haynes
Tracey Heber
Heather Hefter
Andrea
Heidebrecht
Christa Held
Heather
Henderson
Angela
Henderson Orr
Melissa
Hendrickson
Dana Herndon
Linda Hibner
Kate Hight-Clark
Elizabeth Hijar
Connie Hill
Rachel Hill
Carrie Himel
Ashlie Hogan

Brandee Holland
Channin Hoover
Sarah Hoover
Brianna Houston
Gwendolyn Howes
Anastasia Huffman
Shea Hughes
Heather Hughes
LaRae Humes
Julie Humphries
Katie Hurst
Jessica Hurtt
Elizabeth Huston
Amanda Hutson
Shannon Imel
Lesley Islas
Darcie Jackson
Holly Jackson
Marie Jackson
Ronna-Renee
Jackson
Maribeth Jacobson
Heather Ann
James
Heather Jenkins
Amanda Johnson
Jill Johnson
Kelly Johnson
Laura Johnson
Morgan Johnson
Becky Johnston
Leanne Johnston
Amanda Jones
Amity Jones
Christine Jones
Melissa Jorgensen
Cara Joyner
Pamela Justus
Stephanie Kandray
Eva Keener
Amy Keffer
Helen Kerr
Tammie Kidd

ACKNOWLEDGMENTS

Rebecca Kiger
Michelle Kime
Jana King
Lauren King
Megan Kinser
Pam Kinser
Shannon Kitchen
Katie Kleinjung
Jennifer Kleparek
Cherilyn Klomp
Barbara Knepper
Leslie Knight
Kimberly Knudsvig
Aundi Kolber
Melody Kopp
Cindy Kreassig
Shawna Kurth
Rebecca LaCount
Maggie Laird
April Lambiotte
Lindsay Langdon
Grace Langer
Beth Latshaw-Foti
Rachel Lawrence
Karen Laywell
Anna LeBaron
Amanda Lee
Gloria Lee
Robin Lee
Ticcoa Leister
Christy LeRoy
KariAnn Lessner
Brandy Lidbeck
Candace Lierd
Jan Liles
Jaime Linder
Joani Livingston
Stephanie Lloyd
Meredith Locker
Vicki Lodder
Heather Long
Julie Long
Megan Lowmaster

Jackie Lumpkin
Abbie Mabary
Kathy Macheras
Deedra Mager
Donna Mahoney
Cathleen Maloney
Kate Mardis
Rebekah Johnson
  Maricelli
Bethany Marlow
Dana Martin
Jeanna Martin
Carroll Marxen
Anna Maschke
Tracy Massey
Emily Mastrantonio
Kelley Mathews
Melinda Mattson
Sarah May
Michele Mayhan
Jinny McCall
Kristi McClellan
Cara McConnell
Crissy McDowell
April McGrew
Kara McLendon
Lauren McMinn
Jody McMurrin
Karen McVey
Kelly Meehan
Sally Mellinger
Nancy Messinger
Kande Milano
Taylor Millender
Amanda Miller
Christianna Miller
Kelsey Miller
Maggie Miller
Melissa Miller
Rebecca Miller
Brittany Miller
  Mancill
Cindy Milner

Jill Mitchell
Erin Moffitt
Monica Montoya
Angie Mood
Sherry Mora
Noelle Morin
Cheryl Moses
Lori Motal
Jenny Mrochek
Rosanna Mullet
Claire Mummert
Katie Mumper
Laura Murray
Aline Nahhas
Wendy Navel
Erin Needham
Melinda Nelson
Jennifer Nelson
Lindsey Nihart
Shalimar Niles
Amberly Noble
Jacey Nordmeyer
Fawnda Norman
Celine Noyes
Courtney Oakes
Audra Ohm
Sheila O'Rear
Amber O'Toole
Luain Packard
Heather Parker
Julia Parker
Micaleah Parker
Pam Parker
Jaclyn Parsons
Catherine
  Passmore
Stephanie Patel
Amy Paulson
Theresa Penev
Lindsay Pentecost
Kirsten Petro
Amy Phipps
Allison Pickett

Loyce Pickett
Barbara Pitt
Kacy Pleasants
Ashley Pooser
Kimberly Poovey
Anna Price
Deidre Price
Michelle Prichard
Casey Purnhagen
Megan Quiggle
Jenni Quinn
Cheri Rainer
Sara Rains
Delia Ramsey
Kate Rankin
Suzanne Rees
Amanda Regas
Pattie Reitz
Anna Rendell
McKinley Rich
Jill Richardson
Tesa Riddle
Melissa Ried
Becky Ritta
Stefanie Ritz
Kathi Roach
Stephanie Roberts
Michelle Robinson
Macy Robison
Melody Roebuck
Melissa Roetzel
Tara Rooks
Kristin Rosenbaum
Katelyn Roskamp
Elizabeth Rosner
Jenny Ross
Kelly Ruark
Anna Rubin
Jennifer Ruble
Linda Sanchez
Tiffany Sanchez
Amilee Sanders
Bree Sapp

ACKNOWLEDGMENTS

Elizabeth Sawczuk
Robin Sayers
Amanda Schafer
Breanne Schafer
Heidi Schmidt
Dena Schneider
Erica Schreiber
Elizabeth
    Schulenburg
Sarah Schultz
Kate Scoggins
Melissa Scroggins
Barb Seidle
Jessica Sellers
Betsy Shaak
Erin Shafer
Kelly Shank
Tamara Shope
Julie Shreve
Charity Simpson
Raleen Sloan
Natalie Slusser
Donna Smit
Kelly Smith
LeeAnna Smith
Liz Smith
Sheila Smude
Keri Snyder
Shawna Soto
Jennifer Spills-
    Davis
Brenna Staats

Jennifer Stacy
Mary Stagner
Brenna Stanaway
Courtney Stennett
Kristin Stewart
Sandy Stewart
Lori Stilger
Aubrey Stout
Sheila Stover
Morgan Strehlow
Ann Stritt
Rose Stroemer
Joana Studer
Jody Leigh
    Stufflebean
J'Layne Sundberg
Pat Sutton
Torrey Swan
Ruth Szpunar
Carmel Tajonera
Jenna Taylor
Shannon Taylor
Ashley Thomas
Kibbie Thomas
Beth Thompson
Carrie Beth Tigges
Judy Tompkins
Amanda Torres
Johanna Trainer
Kirsten Trambley
Melanie Traver
Embo Tshimanga

Cristy Tucker
Lori Turnbow
Emily Tuttle
Robin Tutwiler
Abby Twarek
Denise Tyriver
Michelle Unwin
Katie Vale
Penni Van Horn
Erin Vande Lune
Jodi Vanderhoof
Rachel Vasquez
Bethany Vaughn
Nicole Vavra
Brenda Veinotte
Alicia Vela
Jenny Veleke
Perri Verdino-Gates
Tami Vigesaa
Karli Von herbulis
Stephanie Vos
Camille Walker
Rachel Walker
Beth Walker
Jenny Warren
Erin Waters
Holly Waugh
Beth Webb
Melinda Wedding
Karmen Weddle
Melissa Weimer
Sarah Weir

Whitney Werling
Courtney West
JJ West
Erin Wevers
Kristin White
Annie White
    Carlson
Jessica Whitley
Kimberly Widmer
Amy Wiebe
Krista Wilbur
Amy Wilkins
Jennifer Willerton
Linda Willett
Kara Williams
Carrie Williford
Laurel Williston
Joan Brichacek
    Wilson
Jemelene Wilson
Annaliese Wink
Amanda Wissmann
Jessica Wolfe
Erin Woods
Mandy Wren
Jeane Wynn
Curtis Yates
Anita Yaussi
Lori Young
Becky Yurisich
Carmen Zeisler
Lindsay Zielonka

NOTES

EPIGRAPH
1. Louisa May Alcott, *Little Women*, Amy in chapter 44.

CHAPTER 1: FULL PAGE QUOTE
1. Brennan Manning, *The Ragamuffin Gospel* (Colorado Springs: Multnomah, 2000), 157, 159.

CHAPTER 1: UNBRANDED
1. Jen Hatmaker, *Interrupted* (Colorado Springs: Navpress, 2009), 29.
2. "The Everlasting Man Quotes," Goodreads, accessed February 22, 2017, https://www.goodreads.com/work/quotes/2420302.

CHAPTER 2: FULL PAGE QUOTE
1. "Jill Churchill quotes," ThinkExist.com, http://thinkexist.com/quotation/there_is_no_way_to_be_a_perfect_mother-and_a/174966.html.

CHAPTER 4: FULL PAGE QUOTE
1. Oscar Wilde, *The Importance of Being Earnest* (Mineola, NY: Dover, 1990), 8.

CHAPTER 5: FULL PAGE QUOTE

1. This quote is attributed to C. S. Lewis, Lena Horne, and Lou Holtz. Research showed that it does not belong to Lewis but has been quoted by both Horne and Holtz.

CHAPTER 6: FULL PAGE QUOTE

1. Jane Austen, *Mansfield Park* (New York: Penguin, 1996), 217.

CHAPTER 7: FULL PAGE QUOTE

1. "Quote by Laura Ingalls Wilder," *Quotery*, accessed January 4, 2017, http://www.quotery.com/quotes/home-is-the-nicest-word-there-is/.

CHAPTER 8: FULL PAGE QUOTE

1. "George Sand Quotes," BrainyQuote, accessed January 4, 2017, https://www.brainyquote.com/quotes/quotes/g/georgesand143443.html.

CHAPTER 9: FULL PAGE QUOTE

1. Hannah Hutyra, "107 Audrey Hepburn Quotes That Will Inspire You," KeepInspiring.me, accessed January 4, 2017, http://www.keepinspiring.me/audrey-hepburn-quotes/.

CHAPTER 10: FULL PAGE QUOTE

1. Wikipedia, s.v. "Arthur O'Shaughnessy," last modified December 24, 2016, https://en.wikipedia.org/wiki/Arthur_O'Shaughnessy. "Ode" was first published in 1873 and quoted by Willy Wonka in *Willy Wonka & the Chocolate Factory*.

CHAPTER 11: FULL PAGE QUOTE

1. "Dr. Seuss Wisdom Quotes," accessed January 4, 2017, http://www.wisdomquotes.com/quote/dr-seuss-2.html.

CHAPTER 12: FULL PAGE QUOTE

1. "Zora Neale Hurston Quotes," Brainy Quote, https://www.brainyquote.com/quotes/quotes/z/zoranealeh132700.html.

CHAPTER 12: SANCTUARY

1. Anne Lamott, *Bird by Bird* (New York: Anchor Books, 1995), 22. Anne attributes this to her "priest friend Tom."

CHAPTER 13: FULL PAGE QUOTE

1. "Joan Rivers Quotes," Brainy Quote, accessed January 4, 2017.

CHAPTER 14: FULL PAGE QUOTE

1. "Agatha Christie Quotes," Brainy Quote, accessed January 4, 2017, http://www.brainyquote.com/quotes/quotes/a/agathachri401066.html.

CHAPTER 15: FULL PAGE QUOTE

1. "I Used to Be Snow White, But I Drifted," Quote Investigator, June 29, 2013, http://quoteinvestigator.com/2013/06/29/snow-drift/.

CHAPTER 15: DOLDRUMS

1. Dictionary.com, http://www/dictionary.com/browse/doldrums.

CHAPTER 16: FULL PAGE QUOTE

1. "Football Quotes," Sports Feel Good Stories, accessed January 4, 2017, www.sportsfeelgoodstories.com/football-quotes/.

CHAPTER 17: FULL PAGE QUOTE

1. "Phylicia Rashad Quotes," Brainy Quote, accessed January 4, 2017, /www.brainyquote.com/quotes/quotes/p/phyliciara504113.html.

CHAPTER 18: FULL PAGE QUOTE

1. Anne Lamott, Facebook post, April 8, 2015 at 4:31p.m., https://m.facebook.com/AnneLamott/posts/662177577245222.

CHAPTER 18: FORGIVENESS SCHOOL

1. Brennan Manning, *The Ragamuffin Gospel* (Colorado Springs: Multnomah, 2005), 40.

2. "Henri J.M. Nouwen Quotes," Goodreads, accessed January 4, 2017, https://www.goodreads.com/quotes/1625.

CHAPTER 19: FULL PAGE QUOTE

1. "Benjamin Franklin Quotes," Brainy Quote, accessed February 24, 2017, https://www.brainyquote.com/quotes/quotes/b/benjaminfr132175.html. Benjamin Franklin sent a letter written in French to his friend Monsieur L'Abbé Morellet (André Morellet) that discussed wine and God. In 1818 William Temple Franklin, who was the grandson of Benjamin, published a posthumous collection of the statesman's letters based on the originals.

CHAPTER 20: FULL PAGE QUOTE

1. "St. Thomas Aquinas," The Preterist Archive, accessed January 4, 2017, http://www.preteristarchive.com/StudyArchive/a/aquinas-thomas.html.

CHAPTER 21: FULL PAGE QUOTE

1. "Sophie Tucker Quotes," ThinkExist.com, accessed January 4, 2017, http://thinkexist.com/quotation/from_birth_to_age-a_girl_needs_good_parents-from/263341.html.

CHAPTER 22: FULL PAGE QUOTE

1. Toni Morrison quote from *Beloved*, Good Reads, accessed February 26, 2017, http://www.goodreads.com/quotes/1056996-grown-don-t-mean-nothing-to-a-mother-a-child-is.

CHAPTER 23: FULL PAGE QUOTE

1. "Helen Keller Quotes," Brainy Quote, accessed February 26, 2017, https://www.brainyquote.com/quotes/quotes/h/helenkelle109208.html.

ABOUT THE AUTHOR

Jen Hatmaker is the author of the *New York Times* bestseller *For the Love* (plus eleven other books) and happy hostess of a tightly knit online community where she reaches millions of people each week. She is a high-functioning introvert who lives her home life in yoga pants and her travel life in fancy yoga pants. She and her husband, Brandon, founded the Legacy Collective, a giving community that granted more than a million dollars in its first year and funds sustainable solutions to systemic problems locally and globally. They also starred in the popular series *My Big Family Renovation* on HGTV and stayed married through a six-month remodel. Jen is a mom to five, a sought-after speaker, and a delighted resident of Austin, Texas, where she and her family are helping keep Austin weird. For more information, visit jenhatmaker.com.